CW00554916

CLEAR GOALS

What Do You Really Want to Achieve in Life?

Ultimate Success Through Personal Goal Planning in 4 Steps

by

Patrick Drechsler

© Copyright 2021 – All rights reserved.

The content contained in this book may not be reproduced, duplicated or transmitted without the direct written permission of the author or publisher.

Under no circumstances will the publisher or author be blamed or held legally responsible for any damages, recovery or financial loss due directly or indirectly to the information contained in this book.

Legal notice:

This book is copyrighted and intended for personal use only. The reader may not modify, distribute, sell, use, quote, or paraphrase any of the contents of this book without the permission of the author or publisher.

Disclaimer:

The information contained in this document is for educational and entertainment purposes only. Every effort has been made to provide accurate, current, reliable and complete information. No warranties of any kind are stated or implied.

Readers acknowledge that the author is not providing legal, financial, medical or professional advice. By reading this document, the reader agrees that under no circumstances will the author be liable for any direct or indirect loss arising from the use of the information contained in this document, including but not limited to errors, omissions or inaccuracies.

Table of Contents

Introduction

Imagine this: You've just resolved to earn money on top of your low-paying job. It is supposed to be your way off the hamster wheel that you are currently trapped on doing a job every day that pays poorly, and that you can't stand. So, you take on a weekend job working on the black in a restaurant to increase your income. But after only 3 weeks you are physically and mentally drained because the workload is simply too much for you. You start showing up irregularly for your side job, get fired, and you're back to square one again. Only this time you feel much worse, because in addition to disliking your main job, you're physically and mentally exhausted. This is a classic case of **_setting too many or too high goals for yourself._**

Another scenario: You are about to embark on a new phase of your life. You've got your high school diploma in the bag with a fabulous average of 1.0. Your teachers predict an outstanding future for you. You are feeling happy enjoying your free time after graduation, but you know that important decisions have to be made soon: Study/training, or a relaxing year abroad? The latter appeals to you because you want to explore the world and don't know which course of study is right for you at the moment anyway. Your parents however urge you to study Medicine right away. They are proud of you and just decide what is best for you from their point of view. You're not even remotely convinced, because being a doctor doesn't match your actual desires for the future, but you decide to go for it anyway. The result: dropping out of college, angry parents, and you as a disillusioned and indecisive dropout who spent 2 years of his life doing something that didn't live up to expectations. Even though you knew beforehand that it would be the wrong path, you did it anyway and messed up a promising future. This is a classic case of ***setting the wrong goals or letting other people influence your goals too much.***

Goal setting is an art in itself. Those who master it increase their likelihood of succeeding many times over. The opposite is true when your goals are not set correctly: too high goals, too many goals, not following one's actual interests and dreams, being influenced too much by other people, showing little motivation and discipline as a result of setting the wrong goals ... these cases are very likely to lead to failure. Although it is obvious, unfortunately a surprising number of people make these mistakes over and over again. Have you noticed people in your circle of acquaintances doing things they don't really want to do? Have you observed how some people pursue such a large number of goals that they can't manage it and fail? Do you often hear people around you complain that they don't like what they do? And most importantly, are similar things happening in your *own* life?

It's time you started setting your goals properly with the highest probability of success; I say *with the highest probability* because there are no guarantees that you will achieve your goals. But here comes a fascinating message for you: as long as you pursue goals that are truly in line with your dreams, it is not always necessary to actually achieve them. Because by simply pursuing them, you fill your life with motivation, purpose, enthusiasm, and fascination anyway. Even with the most successful people goals are sometimes dropped because life develops and evolves in equally interesting different directions.

But whatever your goals in life, and whatever is closest to your heart's desires – this guidebook will give you valuable, authentic assistance and suggestions based on my extensive experience in the matter. Goal setting is an important area of personal development and I want to make sure you get it right. Through a unique fusion of personal development and business management techniques that came about one day when I noticed, during a review of my business studies, that a significant part of business administration is devoted to the question of the ideal objective. When I took a closer look at the content, I was thrilled. *Surely this high level of precision and fine subdivision of goals can also apply to people in their everyday lives!* was my thought at the time. When I combined areas of goal setting and planning from my business studies, with my life experiences, I was thrilled with the benefits I achieved, from my personal life to my family to my hobbies and career. Do you want to set and achieve your goals in a clear step-by-step sequence, with really precise methods? Then you've come to the right place! This guide offers you completely original methods that work, as my own life experience demonstrates.

When it comes to goal setting, there are 2 factors that really matter: first, there are the things you have to do – the **obligations**. Then there is the space you have free for planning, in which you set your **desired goals**. After the introductory first chapter, chapters 2 and 3 will teach you how to correctly plan your commitments and desired goals, step by step, with the help of 2 lists which you refine following the tips on filtering, laid out in Chapter 4, and long-term planning in Chapter 5. It's kind of like your own personal life guide. In between the main sections, there are plenty of hints on how to find suitable goals, what you should pay attention to in your environment and other important elements to help you perfect your goal setting skills. The tasks in the chapters and the big final task at the end of each chapter will help you to put the theory into practice.

Planning your goals lets you live every dream precisely!

This guidebook is unique because the inspiration for it came in an unusual way. But equally unusual – at least at first glance – was the path I took to optimize my own goal setting achievements.

The foundation for my success with various goals and plans was my business studies. Then I poured through numerous guidebooks and listened to courses from many coaches, but for a long time nothing could help me to properly formulate my ideas. Then one day I held a book from my former business studies in my hand, and it came to me. This idea led me to the perfect way of dealing with goals. Now I pass this idea, that runs like a thread through the entire book, on to you. I hope it will help you, as it has helped me.

So, what is this idea? If you look at business administration and study company objectives as an essential part of entrepreneurial activity, you will find that companies are **systems**. From this realization follows important insights for goal setting. While reading about the subject, it dawned on me that exactly the same applies to people. You and your environment – you are a system! If you internalize this and all the consequences that follow from it, you will have the ability to set goals optimally and keep the probability of achieving them at its highest.

Don't worry: You won't be dehumanized in this book, when being treated like a business. You'll just learn how to harness the enormous precision of successful corporations in goal setting – for your job, for your personal life, for your social contacts, for your hobbies, for your dreams, and so much more! The most powerful and famous corporations achieve most of their goals because they plan everything meticulously. Now imagine if you did the same as a human being: accurate planning, high precision, yet plenty of room for spontaneity and unforeseen events – you would be living your dreams. Let's start today!

Man, and his environment as systems

By definition, a system is a whole composed of several parts. These parts connect with each other so that there are constant interactions. It follows that when you act, it affects multiple parts of the system, from which you expect a certain improvement to occur.

Now imagine that you achieve your intended improvement. Perhaps it has the desired effect, but at the same time affects another area of life in a way that is not desired? Besides this, it could be that an action doesn't only produce that one expected improvement. Instead, 2 or 3 additional improvements occur in other areas of life that you would not have expected. All the greater would then be the joy. So, in a nutshell, *many of the goals you achieve have multiple effects, not just the one you planned.*

What parts are present in the "life" system? Of which parts is your personal system composed? On the one hand it is you, on the other hand it is your environment. Imagine how much these

2 parts make up already – just you yourself consist of hundreds, maybe thousands of other parts. You see what I mean? Sometimes your inner critic wants to bring your system out of balance. But if you overcome your inner critic, you are happy to have fulfilled a duty and not to have postponed it. In the evening, after a hard day you are tired, but your wife and children are waiting for you in top form. Wife and children – other parts of the system you have to consider. With every little decision or act you perform certain parts of the system start moving. How are you supposed to keep track of it?

Example

You have ambitious professional goals. These start with a degree, then move into your first few years of work, and finally culminate in a doctorate. The result is even more appointments, duties and opportunities that you don't want to miss. You already know during your studies that the most salient features of your daily life will be a full schedule. What makes it tough is the family life on top of your professional activities: How can a person with so many work commitments have a happy family life? It is possible, no question! But it is difficult; more difficult, at least, than for a person who doesn't have a 12-hour workday followed by appointments. This is probably the most common way in which the system characteristics of a person's life show up: Work or family? Sometimes it's hard to balance both. If both are your goal, early planning is required to successfully manage a life with both career and family.

Any person who sets more than one goal in their life faces the challenge of balancing between mutually influencing factors. This also influences your daily routines. Let's assume that a person doesn't want to prioritize between work and family: something like this can go well for a while until, before an important professional lecture, a call comes that their child is seriously ill in hospital. What decision is made now? The person decides to take care of the child and the next day has to hand in his or her notice because a deal has fallen through due to the missed lecture, resulting in high sales losses for the company.

So, for you a central factor in goal setting is prioritization. Which goal is more important in general terms? Which goal is more important depending on the reality at this particular moment? A person who works with tunnel vision towards only one thing has a much easier time of it. They don't have to weigh up different goals. A balancing act between family and work is avoided because she has already committed herself to one thing. This person strictly follows her path and disregards side effects. While she also lives in a system, she doesn't care about the interactions. Perhaps she is even willing to go over dead bodies, although that would be an extreme case.

People who pursue a single goal with tunnel vision can be very successful; temporarily. In the long run, however, this lifestyle produces negative side effects. For example, tunnel vision leads to overlooking opportunities for synergy between different goals. Few new things are tried. Possibly, the physical and psychological strain is so strong that burnout occurs at some point as well.

Tunnel vision is not the rule. Most of the time, people have multiple dreams. Or they have dreams *and* obligations, which require the pursuit of several goals at the same time. This results in the elementary challenge for you, which this guidebook would like to help you with. You live in a system. One part of this system is you with everything that belongs to you. The other part of this system is your environment; likewise, with everything that belongs to *it*. Your goal is to bring transparency into your system, or to get clarity about it in the first place, i.e., to find goals that are important for you, that can realistically be fulfilled according to the current circumstances. After that, the trick will be to pursue these goals in coordination with everything that surrounds you. Only in this way can the entire system, i.e., your life, function according to your dreams.

There are no simple *if-then* principles in life. In most cases, a decision not only results in the desired effect, but also in additional (side) effects. Big players in companies are aware of this. Therefore, no decisions are ever made on a whim. There are no ill-considered actions. There is less risk of negative surprises afterwards. Of course, companies have certain advantages because decisions are usually made in consultation with several people. Emotional decisions are highly unlikely in teams of several people and are not found at all in the largest companies.

You can acquire these qualities yourself as well. A key factor in avoiding decisions that are too spontaneous, emotionally driven, or based purely on luck, is controlling emotional impulses. If you have read my book *Stop Procrastination Immediately*, it offers plenty of methods to help you do this very effectively.

My experience

How much we humans are part of a system of interactions, I got to experience first-hand when I joined a new circle of friends via a work colleague. It was completely different from what I had been used to. The looseness of my new "friends" fascinated me. However, the same looseness had the disadvantage of exposure to a constant use of clichés, outdated role models, and other unwise expressions. Why these people had such a strong attraction to me, I still can't answer to this day. But they did. Over time, I adapted their ways of thinking to some extent. My interpersonal skills and previous discipline faded. Today, I am fortunately out of that environment, which did not suit me. But I would never have thought that my character would change so much in the meantime due to a different environment. It had an impact on everything I did and thought.

First: Find the right goals

Basically, this whole book and each of the 4 steps presented is about this one thing: finding the right goals. Once you have the right goals, you will have ...

> ➤ analyzed your system and identified the interactions.
> ➤ Knowledge of how you react to the potential interactions.
> ➤ Prioritized the most important goals over the less important ones.
> ➤ Followed what is close to your heart.
> ➤ Developed motivation, discipline and consistency as you follow your dreams and create the best conditions for achieving them.

These aspects and more will be ensured once you have found the right goals. Because "right" means nothing other than that: you will know what corresponds to your dreams while at the same time taking your system into account. For example, if you have a spouse, it's important to agree on certain goals together so that there's a common thread. The same applies to circles of friends. Setting goals is therefore not always a matter for one person but is sometimes linked to the interests of others too.

This guide also teaches you how to involve other people in goal setting where necessary. In order to be able to formulate and pursue goals adequately, you need to understand the word "goal" as precisely as possible. A few words about this ...

The waiter of life: What do you really want?

Welcome to the life restaurant! Here you really get everything you want, as long as it comes from this world and is formulated correctly. So, let's go! You hang up your coat and are glad to be in the warm. The fireplace gives you comfort, and the piano player provides the appropriate background music on this fantastic evening. Today you get what you want from life!

You sit down. After a short while the waiter approaches you. "Can I help you?" he asks you, his notepad and pen ready in hand.

You reply, "I'm hungry. I want to eat."

The waiter repeats his question, "Can I help you?"

You repeat, more forcefully this time, "I want to eat!"

In response, the waiter slowly shakes his head and says he'll give you some more time to think about it until you really know what you want. To help you, he gives you the menu, although it's actually unnecessary. After all, in the life restaurant you get everything you want! Then the waiter leaves and turns his attention to the other guests.

You watch him and the other guests as they exchange. They actually get everything they want. On top of that, the waiter is friendlier to them than to you. Has the whole world conspired against you? What's going on here? You look at the menu and you are shocked: In this restaurant, anything really is possible! It's almost like it's an impertinence that you can't decide.

Sooner than you would like, the waiter comes back to you. He inquires again about your wish. What now? You go by the process of elimination and answer hesitantly, "Well ... I don't want all the meat dishes. I eat vegetarian."

The waiter makes a note of this and is already gone. Before you know it, not only does the waiter return, but a whole entourage comes with him. Both the waiter and his entourage are carrying plates. You wonder why there are so many plates. Have they prepared everything for you that is vegetarian? That would be too much!

In fact, it becomes more paradoxical ... "Here you go," the waiter speaks as he and his entourage place all the plates on your table, "here you have all the meat dishes that are on our menu. And our menu is big because we are the restaurant of life." He smiles.

While the smell of pork knuckles and chicken legs, rises to your nose and the waiter smiles provocatively at you, you lose your nerve: "Why do I get exactly what I didn't want?!?" you ask loudly and excitedly.

The waiter is not aware of his mistake: "I'm sorry, but my time is precious. I don't work on the exclusion principle. What you think about and what you say, that's what you get. I don't pay attention to individual unimportant words."

You understand and then just want a Diet Coke because you're sick of everything. The Diet Coke is served to you a little later. While you are content with it, the people around you are already devoting themselves to the 3rd and

4th courses of their menu. They help each other with their orders and sometimes even with emptying the plate.

Author: Fabian Ries (https://www.fabianries.de/)

Life is just like this restaurant. You have an incredible number of choices. If it seems absurd to you that a person would sit down in a restaurant and just say that they want to eat, realize that this is exactly what happens in real life. Haven't you ever said you wanted something, but weren't specific enough about it? Be honest with yourself:

➢ I want to be rich.
➢ I want to be successful.
➢ I want to be attractive / pretty.
➢ I want to have more friends.
➢ I want to have more career prospects.

Here's the problem: Where is it formulated what wealth, success, etc. mean and what exactly has to be done to achieve it? If you define wealth in terms of money or assets, then you should specify what sum you are aiming for. This already makes it more concrete. Next, the challenge arises that such large and general goals cannot be achieved in the first go. Of course, it is possible to achieve them over the course of several years. But why then burden yourself with a single large goal instead of setting smaller intermediate goals? A division into intermediate goals favors greater motivation. After all, achieving intermediate goals shows progress.

Precision in formulation. Subdivision of major goals into smaller goals. Determination to want to implement the respective goal. These are some of the things that there is hardly any way around when it comes to precise goal formulation. Life is the biggest restaurant in the world with the biggest menu imaginable from which every person has to choose. You are probably aware that every restaurant that does well expands over time. Or at least it expands its offer. So, it is with the life restaurant. This brings us to a typical problem of today's age in setting goals: oversupply.

Today's challenges in setting goals

Developments in recent decades and years have created a wealth of opportunities. These opportunities are expanding prospects for many people. The Internet has created new opportunities for earning money. Becoming self-employed with your own business or as a freelancer is no longer necessarily associated with a high financial outlay. Rent for stores and thus high running costs can be omitted. At this point many councilors are advising you to make money on the Internet. But as much expertise as these guides may contain, they are also very specific: not every person defines success in terms of higher earnings. Even if this were the case, it would not necessarily follow that the models presented in the guidebooks would appeal to the respective reader.

In addition to opportunities for self-employment or in the professional field, a plethora of opportunities have arisen for young people to shape their lives after leaving school. Taking over a parent's business or job as in the past, is no longer the norm. Young people can choose between a lot of training and study programs. As well as study abroad programs so they can explore the world. Hiking through New Zealand for 6 months or rather working with professional rangers at a wildlife park in South Africa? It's all within the realm of possibility. These things are not only available to young adults from the wealthy class of society. Because Germany is a welfare state, there are numerous support programs that young people from other countries can only dream of in a global comparison: State sponsorship for studies and training, State sponsorship abroad, scholarships, organized work & travel and much more!

There is even a wide range of political opinions. Numerous political currents have emerged, so that it is now possible to find exactly the one that fits one's own ideas. Meetings are easy due to the Internet and social media. And there are also numerous directions and movements among religions. Within Christianity alone, there are many diverse forms. The Protestant and Catholic denominations are accompanied by various other groups and sects.

The most diverse choices, philosophies of life and convictions meet. Although much of it has the same core, it is also so very different! And between all this, there you stand, and you have to make decisions. As you age, your options might reduce. Certain things are no longer accessible (e.g., study abroad programs for young people) or become unrealistic (e.g., education). But even for those over 40 with family as well as work responsibilities, a number of new opportunities have recently emerged that were unthinkable a few decades ago.

Example

Start trading stocks at the age of 60? Isn't that already too old? And as a woman too? "Pah, all prejudices!" thought Beate Sanders correctly when she started investing money in shares at the age of 60. She started with the equivalent of 30,000 euros and turned it into a fortune of around 2.5 million euros within 20 years. Her success gave her enormous status and made it clear that investing in stocks is realistic for anyone. She wrote books and participated in interviews, until in September 2020, she died of cancer at the age of 82.

So, perspectives are always there. Ordinary people write amazing stories. Sometimes they become famous. Sometimes it's enough for them to become happy. Most of all, people try new things to experience extraordinary things. Then they set their first goals. Once these are achieved, they move on step by step, raising the bar with each subsequent goal.

I hope I've managed to convince you that *you can really have everything you want*. The only thing is that you must plan your goals correctly and precisely, which brings us to the subject of this chapter. Planning your life and dividing it into stages will assure you reach your objectives as you move from one point to the next. But first we must determine how high your goals should even be. Everything that can't be planned, at least to some extent, is unattainable for the time being, but that will change as we go along. When updating your goals, you will notice when a previously unattainable goal comes closer to you. Then you will make changes. **At the beginning of your goal setting, it is important that you only set plannable and therefore achievable goals**. More about this in the following chapters. But everything that can be realistically planned, you can also implement. Let's say you realized this at the age of 16, then your path to becoming a millionaire would theoretically be a very simple one:

- ➢ Cram hard in school and get a 1.0 average.
- ➢ Graduate medicine with top grades and start working as a doctor.
- ➢ With average annual earnings of 60,000 euros per year, 1 million euros accumulates in less than 20 years.

That sounds too simple? But things *are* just as simple in theory! If there are no breakdowns and you consistently implement your goals, it is just as simple in practice. We will go in-depth in the rest of this book to help you set the goals that you really care about and no matter how high and how far away they are, you will be able to achieve them over time with as high a probability of success as possible. And one thing is sure: *You will find the answers within yourself.* No one can make the decision for you if you are wavering between multiple goals or options. Other people can advise you, but decisions about goals that concern only you, are only yours to make. With that comes the fact that you have to bear the responsibility for them too.

Hint!

Responsibility is a critical point. People who are not used to taking responsibility tend to lead an alienated life. The reason for this assertion is as follows: If you have to make a decision, but it is difficult for you, you ask others. If you are unsure or afraid of the matter in question, you can shift the responsibility to the person who advised you. Being able to shift responsibility may provide some peace of mind. But it does not help you to lead a self-determined life and to realize your dreams. Act and take responsibility! It is right now that your self-determined life begins.

Your environment exerts power on you

Your environment and you, you exert great power on each other. You can help or harm each other; whether consciously or unconsciously. Surely you have already had a conversation with a person who had a completely different character or interests to you. You didn't come to a common denominator and didn't feel entirely comfortable with each other. Over time, you would have found common ground and a pleasant relationship, but it didn't happen. Now imagine that there are people who are regularly confronted with such situations: Bullying victims are an extreme case. They find themselves in an environment that is not only antagonistic, but completely destructive. What are the possible effects of this on the person? She feels lonely, inferior, doubt and may even develop psychological problems.

Of course, there are also positive examples: People who can master so many topics of conversation and have such charisma that almost everyone is attracted to them. They are on top of their game, always have company, often have a strong sense of self-confidence and can hope for support in difficult times.

What if you find out that you can be the 2nd person described? It is up to you to build an environment that complements you perfectly. Even from the worst starting position you are able to build up a circle of family, friends and acquaintances in which you, and the people around you, feel good.

Your environment can be both a driver and an obstacle. This guidebook will show you the way to choose an environment that is as suitable as possible for your goals. You will be free to decide which people you allow into your environment. Advantageous are people you can trust and who support you in your plans. Mutual appreciation is of great importance, it should also be reflected in your choice of words, because emotional intelligence is very important.

Final task

The final task for the 1st chapter heralds your change; the change from a person with nothing but fascinating dreams that require a clear direction, to a person with absolutely precise goals and a pathway to their achievement. The first step is to take stock: write down in bullet points all the things that seemed particularly important to you in this chapter. Above all, you should write down things that you had not yet considered. Often the devil is in the details: Maybe the small lessons contain the answers to why you have not yet achieved your goals as you would have liked. Also, note the things that you obviously identify as deficits in yourself to achievement.

Step 1 | What must be?

As much as you may sometimes hate to hear it, *some things have to be done*. They cannot be prevented. Even if you would prefer to stay in bed in the morning, you still don't. Because work, lectures, the crying baby or other obligations make you act to the contrary. So, you do what you have to do. There are other **commitments** too, some of them are even necessary to exist. Others are more or less self-chosen, such as the job or the baby. The job, although self-chosen, is necessary to earn money. The baby needs an education to prepare for childhood and later adolescence and adulthood – this is also clearly a duty.

This chapter will help you identify your commitments and plan for them. Because before you can work on your wishes and dreams, you have to cover your mandatory program. Otherwise, it will be critical for your health, your ability to pay for things, or your family in the worst case. A very important lesson awaits you, one that is key to making your life more relaxed in the long run:

As much as it may seem today that you are trapped in your daily routine and that your obligations will never let you go, this impression is deceptive. Because in the long run, things about your obligations can be changed. This will give you the chance to live the life you dream of. A different job? Better salary? Passive income? A more relaxed family life? All within the realm of possibility, but only in the long term.

Exist

Since time immemorial in the history of living beings, the goal has been to keep one's own species alive. Survival and reproduction served to achieve this objective. Today, both are easier. Survival is no longer a bare struggle, as it may have been in the days of the Neanderthals. Reproduction is assured, even if not every person chooses to have children. Food is available in stores and in most countries the majority of the population can easily afford it. Medical care in Germany is good. Times of crisis, such as the Corona pandemic, have shown how well the German health care system is doing compared to other nations. The fact that it has **become easier to secure one's livelihood** provides **advantages** above all for people in the highly developed industrialized countries:

➢ More time! In the past, a lot of time was spent hunting and farming for people to be able to feed themselves. This time is now saved because food can be easily bought, and farming equipment is efficient. Fast food for fast daily routines also makes things easier for city dwellers.

➢ More safety! A few centuries ago, a simple flu could mean death. Today, diseases can be treated better, and the general life expectancy is increasing.

➢ More education! People are more informed about what happens in the body when a certain vitamin is deficient or what the effects of insufficient sleep are. This can prevent negative consequences for health and psyche.

Now, realize what tremendous advantages you were given when you saw the light of day in this age! Do this with a feeling of gratitude. Because gratitude is a basic building block for approaching life positively.

My experience

I once had a flu-like infection and no paracetamol or other antipyretic at home. On the 2nd day of my infection, my heart, beat over 200 beats a minute for several hours – you can't stand that for long! In fact, with this seemingly banal flu infection, the ambulance service had to come, and I stayed in the hospital for 2 days. In that situation, I at least came close to understanding what a privilege we enjoy by having medications today that completely cure previously fatal infections within a day or 2. In fact, people used to die at the youngest ages because of flu-like infections. Today, by comparison, we have it much better in most places.

Your existence and that of many other people in the German population has improved in the course of the last centuries and even the last decades. Many things have become easier, many things have become better. Of course, there are still inequalities in this country, crimes happen and there are huge income differences between rich and poor. But if you want to look at it optimistically and motivate yourself – and that's what I recommend you do, because it doesn't make sense to slow yourself down – then you come to the realization that things have improved for the low-income earners in society, too. After all, even low-income earners usually have a roof over their heads thanks to government support, their children can at least go to school and learn for a better life as well as work, and it's not uncommon for them to even own a plasma screen with a Netflix subscription to pass the time. It's not the rule, but it does happen. Low-income earners could only dream of this a century ago.

With the conditions of existence improved on the whole, scope opens up for people to ...

> ➤ Work on the quality fulfillment of their existential needs.
> ➤ Restructure here and there.
> ➤ Promote and support their goals.

Existential needs (food, drink, sleep, medical care, security etc.) are the basic building blocks on which all other goals are built. For example, you won't be able to work well if you don't sleep enough and rest doesn't make up the deficit. At worst, you'll make mistakes that cost you your job. Or you may follow through in the long run and keep your job, but eventually suffer mental illness because you overexert yourself. Unhealthy eating is a danger that can even lead to hospitalization or expensive dental surgery, for example.

I have had shocking experiences with the long-term negative effects on the psyche, which still shape my actions today: When I first started my own business, I put all my eggs in one basket. Old-age provision? I can take care of that when I'm older. At a young age, I first have to generate capital and grow my business. Public health insurance? Too expensive for young people, I prefer private health insurance instead. And plenty of sleep? You can catch up on sleep when you're dead I thought. What ultimately turned out to be precarious for me were the latter 2 points: Health insurance and sleep. I responsibly put a retirement plan into action 4 years later and did everything right. But with health insurance, I wasn't very forward-thinking. Although I had a history with my heart, I hid it and cheated my way into the cheaper insurance policy. I slept very little and often worked up to 60 hours at a stretch with the help of caffeine pills and energy drinks. Nothing happened to my heart, but instead to my psyche after about 2.5 years. I was exhausted, but I kept working anyway. At some point, various physical signals came to me, including headaches, digestive problems, and later even dental problems. The stress had caused several ulcers to develop in my mouth. Because I could barely eat, I was losing weight, suffering nutrient deficiencies and weakening my immune system. There I was, with super-cheap private health insurance, but a high annual deductible for medical treatments. I had to fork out large amounts of money for it. When I finally recovered after a year of doctor visits, treatments etc., I was as "wealthy" as when I started, and that's when I decided to become sensible. I focused on recovery and a healthy diet, upgraded my health insurance plan for reasonable benefits, and over the next 4 years got much further than before, because I was clear-headed, my body and psyche were recovered, and I could make the right decisions.

If I were to tell you that the quality of your steak or vegetable ratatouille determines how successful you will be, you would think I was crazy. Fortunately, I don't want to say that. Because lightheartedness and balance include buying the ready-to-eat pizza at the discount store and sitting down at home with your loved ones for a fatty and sinfully lazy evening watching Netflix. Instead, I advocate that it's important to maintain a healthy balance. At the end of the day, it's all the little things that add up and lead to results. If you are, for the most part, healthfully and sustainably meeting your existential needs, you are already doing a lot of things right towards furthering your goals.

Hint!

You picked up a book on setting and achieving goals. Now one of the first things you hear is that you should consider sleeping, eating, and other needs when setting goals. Isn't that missing the point a bit? You'll find that just the opposite is true. You should set aside a lot of time in your daily routine for these needs. If you don't take these needs into account and set yourself too many goals, you will either have to cut back on your sleep or relaxed eating, or you will have to cancel set goals again. So, take the existential needs and the following advice seriously. Your health and goal setting will thank you for it!

How important is the quality?

Quality in meeting existential needs plays a crucial role. Have you ever gotten out of a bed that was too small for you? Did you have muscle and joint pain afterwards? If so, please imagine that you also slept too little. The more often this scenario occurs, the less rested you will be. When it comes to sleep duration, scientists are largely in agreement: 6 to 8 hours of sleep is considered optimal. What's more, 6 to 8 hours even lets you live longer, as the *Ärztezeitung* reports with reference to a mammoth study with no less than 117,000 participants! Frequent sleepers who slept significantly longer than the prescribed amount had the following problems:

➢ physical inertia.
➢ Depression or frequent depressive states.
➢ Cigarette and alcohol consumption.
➢ Hypertension.

Extreme short sleepers, on the other hand, often suffered from diabetes and obesity. Otherwise, few illnesses were observed in short sleepers, except for the accidents. It is obvious that too little sleep weakens concentration.

Sleep duration is a crucial point for sleep quality. It should neither be too long nor too short, both are associated with disadvantages and dangers. For hormone levels, it is best to sleep in the dark, as it is in nature. In addition, the temperature of the room should be taken into account: Between 16 and 19 degrees is considered ideal, as this is the best way to activate the growth hormone somatropin after falling asleep. This hormone influences the repair processes of muscles, skin and hair. The question of a comfortable and ergonomic sleeping surface remains. Comfortable sleeping ensures faster falling asleep and more physical well-being during everyday life. The simplest solution is to buy a mattress and pillows that you find comfortable after a test lie. If you have the desire and the money for a professional solution, you can have the mattress and pillow individually adjusted to your body.

Other authors, such as Calvin Hollywood in his guidebook *Wer will, der kann!* (2018), emphasize the importance of getting enough sleep at the optimal time: *"It's really very, very rare that I ever go to bed after 10 p.m. Yes, there are certainly a few exceptions: when I have a long-haul flight and am traveling overnight, for example, or on New Year's Eve. But in general, my alarm clock rings at 9:30 p.m., telling me that I should now prepare for sleep. My goal is to always get between seven and eight hours of sleep so that I'm really in top shape the following day."*

Notice

Just so you really internalize what we're talking about here: You spend 6 to 8 hours a day sleeping in bed. As you get older, this duration decreases due to your basal metabolic rate decreasing. If you calculate with the 6 to 8 hours for the sake of simplicity, 25 to about 33% of your life takes place in bed! If this part of your life does not get the attention it deserves, the other parts will be negatively affected. Due to interactions (see Chapter 1: Humans and their environment are systems), poor sleep can even negatively affect half of your life. Therefore, take this section on sleep seriously and strive for optimal sleeping conditions.

When it comes to food and drink, with the right nutrition you will feel better, positively influence your health and increase the probability of physical as well as mental performance. The best way to demonstrate this is with the example of an athlete. Athletes need resources, the most important of which is energy. This is provided over a long period of time by carbohydrates. However, not all carbohydrates are the same. The sugar underneath only provides a short energy boost. Long-chain carbohydrates, such as those from whole grains and vegetables, are best for long-term performance. For the athlete, this recommendation may be especially true so that he can complete his marathon, but it also applies to employees in the office. If breakfast consists of only coffee in the morning and you have to polish off a pack of Haribo towards mid-morning to raise performance levels, something has been done fundamentally wrong. Because apart from a short performance boost due to the rapid rise in blood sugar levels, little comes of it later. The diet has no quality. Instead, the foundation for diabetes and obesity is laid.

To ensure quality in nutrition, the easiest way is to follow the 10 rules of the DGE:

1. Eat a variety of foods and, above all, integrate plant-based foods into a varied diet.
2. Eat at least 3 vegetables and 2 fruits daily.
3. Among the cereal products prefer the whole grain versions.
4. Eat milk and dairy products daily, fish up to twice a week and a maximum of 300 to 600 grams of meat a week.
5. Use predominantly vegetable oils to meet fat requirements.
6. Instead of sugar and salt prefer to season with herbs and spices.
7. Drink at least 1.5 liters of water per day. Otherwise, prefer calorie-free or low-calorie drinks, such as tea.
8. Prepare food gently to keep micronutrient content as high as possible.
9. Eat slowly and schedule breaks between meals.
10. Keep an eye on body weight and exercise regularly.

Feel free to read more about this. It is best to use the official websites of recognized institutes or professional literature as sources, because many Internet sources convey the information incompletely or incorrectly. Change your diet step by step. It is not necessary to do a 180° turn. In addition, here and there an exception and a sweet is allowed, because to mortify yourself by unnecessary abstinence does not make sense, as it lowers life enjoyment. A healthy diet optimizes your well-being. Therefore, do not hesitate to make modifications to your current diet slowly so that you feel good.

Well-being is also an existential need because living in pain and restrictions is difficult. You promote well-being through the aforementioned tips on sleep and nutrition. Hygiene and relaxation measures are also important.

Notice

If you've read my book on developing mental strength, you'll be familiar with physical well-being in a different context: Appreciation. Showing appreciation for yourself is a basic building block for becoming satisfied and developing the motivation and confidence needed for the tasks and goals ahead.

You have free choice in the methods you use to enhance your well-being. Relaxation methods such as meditation even have the potential to improve your quality of sleep. Here you can see the interactions that can occur in the human system from a positive point of view: By meditating, you are taking a measure that increases your physical well-being and at the same time boosts the quality of your sleep.

Other measures for increasing physical well-being include massages, stretching exercises, sports, walks, and yoga. In addition, hygiene increases your physical well-being. It is even a crucial part of health. Hygiene and health include, for example, having the recommended professional teeth cleaning twice a year at a dental office. It is the only hygiene measure for healthy people that really requires medical implementation. So, take it especially seriously, because operations on the teeth or even dentures can become necessary sooner than you imagine. This is unpleasant and expensive. It can even affect the achievement of goals immensely. As you can see, it's the little things that make the difference.

Restructuring methods and approaches

Here I have created a list of essential existential needs. Copy it on a sheet of paper and determine your priority commitments for a healthy life as well as estimate the time they would take up in your routine:

Must-Target	Notes	Time required
Sleep		
Nutrition		
Hygiene		
physical well-being		

The good news for you at this point is that you have leeway in scheduling these areas. When it comes to sleep, you can only choose between 6- and 8-hours duration, but at least you have 2 hours of leeway. In terms of food, there are the options to eat healthy convenience food or order in to save time, or to cook for yourself to save money. Now let's go over the methods and approaches to restructuring that help you gain time or quality in your existential needs.

Task 1

After you have transferred the table from above onto a sheet of paper, the work begins. Use the first list to document your behavior so far. Note how much time you have spent on each of the 4 areas each day. If you didn't do something every day, calculate from the week to the day by dividing the hours you devoted to one thing during the week by 7.

In my case, for example, the following picture used to come out:

Must-Target	Notes	Time required
Sleep		10 hours
Nutrition		2 hours
Hygiene		45 minutes
physical well-being		0,5 hours

I saw the biggest deficit in my sleep and physical well-being. I used to get only 0.5 hours of physical relaxation a day. My change was to sleep 2 hours less. This freed up 2 hours, one of which I invested in physical well-being. The other hour I saved to use elsewhere. This is how the following table was created:

Must-Target	Notes	Time required
Sleep		8 hours
Nutrition		2 hours
Hygiene		45 minutes
physical well-being		1,5 hours

Do the same task for yourself. While doing this, think about where you would like to make improvements, for example, to gain more time or invest more time in a better sense of well-being.

This task makes sense but is quite theoretical. In practice challenges arise: How do I implement my aspirations? One popular hurdle is getting up early: How do you manage to get up early? Most of the time, you've gotten into the habit of sleeping too long or sleeping too short. At this point, a challenging path of change awaits you. On the one hand, my book *Habits of Winners* will help you to successfully change habits. On the other hand, the following 3 tips should prove helpful:

1. Proceed step by step. For example, instead of waking up 2 hours earlier immediately, try waking up half an hour earlier for 2 weeks. Then increase to 1 hour, and so on.
2. Set hurdles for bad habits. By making it impossible to practice bad habits, it is much easier to change.
3. Reward yourself for successful small steps to increase your motivation.

As a supplement to this task, here is some information on how you can restructure individual areas: In the area of nutrition, for example, you can increase it if you find that you always have too little time to eat or cook. This will bring more quality and probably more freshness to your diet. If you find that you invest too much time in nutrition, you can think about reducing the quality minimally by buying ready-made food now and then or cooking less fussily. A good option to get food quickly is snacks on the go or deliveries.

Notice

These seemingly small things that you have planned and timed so far (sleep, diet, etc.) will determine whether you have 2 hours more or even 3 hours less each day to work on your dreams. Do not underestimate the importance these things. Because if you do, everything will go back to its usual course: You'll stay stuck in a hamster wheel and miss your goals partially or completely. Your success derives from the fact that you plan exactly and set goals. For this, you create a time frame by planning your existential needs. Especially for long sleepers, a time gain of 2 hours through shorter sleep can work wonders.

Standing firmly with both feet on the ground

Because life is not just about existing (that's the part of your commitments we just discussed), but also about having both feet firmly on the ground, the planning continues: What do you need to have both feet firmly on the ground? What goals do you need to set?

- ➢ Lifestyle financing.
- ➢ Protection into old age.
- ➢ Protection in emergencies.

If you don't have enough money on the side to finance your living without work, a job is necessary for regular income. The fact is: work costs time. Accordingly, work is an integral part of most people's agenda. Retirement and health care are also important, although these usually involve a financial cost instead of a time cost. The importance of retirement planning is especially evident in long-term goals: If you want to be agile and explore the world in your old age, you need a good pension. Protection for emergencies is provided by health insurance, liability insurance against damages and other necessary insurances.

If you are not yet satisfied with your main job, your future pension or other aspects of your life, you can make changes over time. Many individuals who neither achieve their dreams nor set them as a goal give into the misconception that their current job is for all eternity. They see themselves as trapped because they have had the training and have been in that particular job for a long time. But that's not right. As mentioned earlier, you can have anything you want! All you need to do is plan **the right long-term goals**.

A lot can be achieved in the long term

In most cases, it is not possible to change jobs from one day to the next. Let's say you're a painter or a nurse and you're unhappy with your job: today you're working your 8 hours and tomorrow you'll be working the same. You have no realistic chance of changing jobs from one day to the next, except in the unlikely event of winning the lottery. However, if you work towards a change on a part-time basis over the long term and plan it accurately, you are very likely to land your dream job in 5 to 8 years.

My experience

One experience I have already shared in another book in this series is my professional transformation. I must confess that I had it easier than other people. I worked as a lecturer only 3 days a week and still earned a full-time salary, so I couldn't complain. But the job was exhausting. I was constantly lecturing the same content. Opportunities for advancement were limited. So, I looked for change and found it: In addition to my job as a lecturer at the time, I built another self-employed business in online marketing, where I could expand my business any way I wanted. I had a positive vision and finally the courage to leave my previous job and try my luck in online marketing. Thus, over time, I obtained a job that I loved and still love today, as well as prospects that are unlimited.

Online marketing is not for everyone. You probably have a different dream or will find your own personal dream through the exercises in this book. It doesn't have to be your job that you change. You can also focus on other things. For example, you can resolve to no longer burden yourself with rent payments for a roof over your head. For this, you set yourself the goal of financing your own property. This way, your existential obligation of paying rent will eventually no longer be necessary. You eliminate a financial burden and lower your running costs by owning your own property.

So, it may be that today you still have to work 8 hours full time, pay the rent or fulfill other duties that don't suit you. But with a positive vision that is realistically achievable, you will have the chance to change your present situation in the long run. To this end, coming up is a passage that describes the classification of goals according to their time reference.

Time reference of goals

The classification of goals according to time is your key to fundamentally turning your life around. Many of the commitments that you can't change overnight and make you unhappy, don't have to be a long-term part of your life! You have the power to change your future and long-term planning is the key to this.

Companies divide their goals into short, medium, and long-term according to a time reference. The same makes sense with people. In the **short term, obligations** are pursued and as we have already mentioned they cannot be changed overnight. For a large part of the population this primarily includes their current full-time job and financing the roof over their heads. When there is too little money, too little time, or other resources in insufficient quantities, pursuing all of these activities is necessary in the short term. Nevertheless, even in the short term, you can **begin to move life in a different direction with long-term planning.** This means that while you are working your full-time job today, you can enroll in a degree program on the side, and thereby gain qualifications that will bring you closer to your dreams in 3 to 5 years from today.

To give you a better idea of the time horizons for short, medium, and long-term goals, here are a few specifications. There are no universal truths, but in business administration the following classification is generally used:

➢ Short-term goals are those that are to be completed within 1 year.
➢ Medium-term goals are designed to last up to 5 years.
➢ Long-term goals are all goals that involve time horizons of more than 5 years.

This time division can be applied to general life planning. Everything that you have to do now (short term) in order to exist, you do over the course of 1 year. That's why setting short-term goals is critical to long-term success.

In the medium term, on the other hand, up to 5 years is enough time to set the course for a new full-time job, a property or a general improvement in prospects. For example, a part-time degree program can be successfully completed within these 5 years. If it's a 3-year bachelor's degree, then within 5 years it's even possible to start the new job that matches your personal dreams, offers more opportunities for advancement and a better salary.

Lastly, the long-term goals: In 5 years, you can achieve anything that is realistic for your situation. If you are a well-earning employee with 3000 euros net per month, you can become a millionaire in over 5 years; here we are realistically talking about around 15 years. If you want to start a family, long-term planning gives you the chance to find a partner and work out a professional situation that will allow you to provide for your family. It is true that something like family planning can only be done for the long term to a limited extent if a partner has not yet been found. After all, falling in love is often accompanied by coincidences. Nevertheless, you can go out on a limb and set yourself such goals for the long term.

Notice

Even medium-term goals give you a lot of leeway. You would be surprised what people can accomplish within 5 years! Let alone in a period of more than 5 years, the long-term time frame opens up possibilities.

Now, these longer-term perspectives have the risk of unpredictability attached to them. Something can come up even with short-term goals, but these are often made up for within a few days or weeks. This is usually easy to do and plan for. The longer the time horizon, the more unforeseen things can happen, which makes medium and long-term goals difficult to plan for. You should therefore plan more generally for medium and long-term goals and have more time and financial cushion available so that you do not have to turn your entire goal planning upside down for unforeseen problems.

Practical use of the classification of goals according to their time reference

How does all this work in practice? How do you benefit from the classification of goals according to their time reference?

It's simple: First, write down all your commitments that we've talked about so far. You write down how many hours a day you have to spend on sleeping, eating, hygiene, full-time job, etc. and how much money you have to spend on food, rent, retirement plans and important insurances. This will show what you have to invest in your life in the short term and how much money and time is left over.

Next, you can take the medium, and long-term view: **How much of my time and money can I spare now to create my desired future in the medium and long term?** In line with this, you set your medium, and long-term goals: For example, you invest 3 hours a week in further training or start financing a property so that you no longer have to pay rent in the long term.

Your advantage compared to the people who have no idea about the time reference of goals: You have timed your desired future and are already carrying out activities today that you know will help you achieve your dream future in the long term! You plan all of this with concrete figures for the time required and the financial outlay, so that you don't overextend yourself with your goals and the probability of success increases. You will learn all this at the end of the chapter in the big final task. For now, you know what time is all-about and why it is important for you. People who don't have this knowledge – and unfortunately this is true of a significant percentage of people out there – plan without an overview of short, medium, and long-term goals. As a result, they only know subconsciously why they are doing something. As a result, they are less likely to be motivated. Another danger is that people set themselves too many goals because they don't have an overall view. They may set themselves so many goals that they cannot achieve them all under any circumstances.

Vision! See the positive in all the efforts

So far, so good: In the long term, an incredible amount can be changed in your life. If you set long-term goals that match your dreams, you'll be well on your way to living the life of your dreams. Most importantly, you'll be able to develop positive visions of your future. You no longer see yourself in the same place at the office every day until just before you retire. Instead, you see yourself traveling the world professionally or in a practice-oriented job – just as you wish. You can also develop positive visions for your family: Your long-term goals can be family-oriented, so that you and your loved ones manage to go on vacation more often because the financial situation has improved. It's also possible that your children will benefit from unique opportunities, such as studying abroad, because of the better living conditions that you provide.

Whatever long-term goal you set for yourself: Every long-term and concretely named goal that you tackle through your actions today helps you to develop positive visions. These positive visions provide you with tremendous motivation and follow-through. Your life gets a meaning!

Example

There is a speech by Arnold Schwarzenegger (successful bodybuilder, Hollywood actor, entrepreneur, politician) that garnered just over 10 million views. It was one of the speeches that went the most viral in the history of the Internet. He talks about success and about his early days in the US: 5 hours of training, work, university, 4 hours of acting school etc. Here is an interesting excerpt:

People used to ask me when they saw me training [...]: "Why do you train so hard —5 hours a day, 6 hours a day — and still have a smile on your face? The others are training just as hard as you, but they look unhappy. Why is there such a difference?" I used to tell people, "It's different for me: I'm reaching for a goal. Ahead of me is the title of Mr. Universe (biggest award in bodybuilding; note). Every repetition I do brings me closer to achieving that goal; closer to making that goal, that vision, a reality. [...] That's why I couldn't wait to do another 500-pound squat, another 500-pound bench press, another 2,000 sit-ups, another set. So let me tell you this: visualizing your goal and striving for it is fun and enjoyable. You need a goal in your life; no matter what you do in your life.

That's it: Visualize! Visualize your success and everything you do now, which may seem insignificant or puny in itself, will take on an incredibly positive meaning! As you do, you will be more likely to perform your duties consistently and quickly, in order to have more time for your goals and your dream future.

So, when you create a life plan, you make it up of small, short-term goals and larger medium, or long-term goals. The medium and long-term goals are always subject to change and adjustment. Just because you are currently doing a job that you may not like does not mean that this will be the case permanently. Therefore, in the medium and long term, every minute you can spare, you are working on your dream future!

The overall motivation is as follows: The 8 hours you spend at work today are the key to financing new prospects for yourself or to acquiring important skills for them. An example: A person uses a permanent position for 3 years after her education, although she hates the employer. However, she knows that she will learn a lot there and will then be able to start her own business with a high probability of success.

Internalize one thing: Even with a great dislike for your current commitments, you should be optimistic and focus on your mid, to long-term possibilities. Because these opportunities are your path to achieving your dreams.

Task 2

Long-term goals can be promoted through visualization exercises. You may have read about visualizations in my other books. They are a well-known method in mental and motivational trainings.

In visualizations, you put your goals down on paper in writing or in the form of a graphic. It's best to use intermediate steps: For example, write down the grade point average you are aiming for in your training on a sheet of paper and hang it on a wall at home. That way, you can always keep an eye on your success. This will unlock additional motivation in you. Alternatively, you can use your imagination by visualizing the state you want to achieve: If you close your eyes and imagine several times a day how you will reach the goal and feel the success at the end of a multi-year journey, you will create a positive vision that will make it easier for you to master the individual stages until you reach the goal. Think about and/or research on the Internet 3 visualization methods that appeal to you and support you in achieving your goals. You will work with these methods later.

Attention, the time is limited! Use it!

You probably know the many quotes about taking advantage of the little time you have. After all, at some point it would be too late for that. Some people think that these quotes are just truisms that will fizzles out. But there is a lot of truth behind them. Here are 10 sentences that can be very helpful:

The ten commandments of time

1. It is not too little time that we have, but it is too much time that we do not use. – Lucius Annaeus Seneca
2. When the time comes when one could, the time is over when one can. – Marie von Ebner-Eschenbach
3. Time that we take is time that gives us something. – Ernst Ferstl
4. Time does not pass more quickly than it used to, but we pass it more hurriedly. – George Orwell
5. There are thieves who are not punished and yet steal the most precious thing: time. – Napoleon
6. The people who never have time do the least. – George Christoph Lichtenberg
7. Time lingers long enough for the one who wants to use it. – Leonardo da Vinci
8. We live in a time of perfect means and confused ends. – Albert Einstein
9. Your time is limited, so don't waste it living someone else's life. Don't let dogma trap you. Don't let the opinions of others stifle your inner voice. Most importantly, have the courage to follow your heart and intuition. Everything else is beside the point. – Steve Jobs

10. Ordinary people only think about how they spend their time. An intelligent person tries to take advantage of it. – Arthur Schopenhauer

Each of these quotes expresses, in one way or another, that the time we have is valuable. Orwell and Einstein emphasize typical problems of today's world, that we humans act too fast and too confused, although the available means are actually perfect, and enough time *is* present. Von Ebner-Eschenbach and Steve Jobs ring the alarm bells and warn us to use the time while it is still possible. Steve Jobs formulates in detail that it is necessary to follow one's own goals for this. In doing so, one should not let oneself be lured into a trap by dogmas. These dogmas are sometimes the thieves of time that Napoleon addresses in his quote: dogmas and people are thieves who rob people of their precious time and go unpunished. Seneca and da Vinci give consideration to the idea that enough time is always present, as long as one really wants to use it. Schopenhauer notes differences among people. Thereby it is a sign of intelligence to use the time and not "only" to spend it – to act meaningfully, purposefully and for a concrete purpose to a concrete benefit.

Some of these quotes are so simplistic that they ignore numerous factors. But that's what can help you think outside the box: For example, I dislike quote VI, which says that people who never have time do the least. It's pretty simplistic in that form, generalizing, and unfair to the many exceptions. But when I think about it a little longer, I develop a particular interpretation of the quote that I can do something with: The quote criticizes the fact that one talks one's way out of certain things; under the pretext of not having time. In reality, however, one does have time. In fact, even today I find situations in which I show this behavior, although it would be better for me not to talk my way out of it and to spend an hour working, reading, doing sports or something similar.

Task 3

You have 10 quotes. Sure, you don't agree with all of them, or you find some unfair. But there is at least a little bit of truth in each one. Write the quotes on the left side of a piece of paper and leave space on the right for comments about them. Afterwards, think about each one. The question you will have to answer for each is: "How can this quote help me improve the way I manage my time so far and thereby further my goals?" The goal here is that you openly consider how you can improve. These quotes will help you to look at things from different angles.

The purpose of this assignment and the explanations given so far is to show you how limited time is in a person's life. Why does this topic belong in this chapter? It's simple: In your life, an incredible amount of time is spent on your obligations! Working, preparing and consuming food, health, keeping your household in order... In fact, these things are a must. I was downright shocked when I observed and recorded over the course of a week how much time even the most ordinary chores take up: Cooking, vacuuming, laundry, ironing, etc. Leaving these things out, however, is not an option. After all, living in disorder, with poor health and eating a lot of convenience food reduces your prospects for the future.

My experience

What should appeal to you at this point is the fact that by consistently working towards your goals, you can buy yourself time. That's what I did when I was drawing a higher income and no longer wanted to completely take care of the household. I still did the ironing, laundry, office stuff and cooking myself. For vacuuming and mopping, on the other hand, I hired help. In the garden, I had a neighbor's boy do the most tedious work for me. He earned 10 euros pocket money every hour and I no longer had to weed or mow the lawn but could finally work on the terrace. By delegating this work, I bought myself about 5 additional hours of time each week. Since my income had increased significantly, I could easily afford it.

You will be able to delegate certain work and gain time. However, this requires accurate planning which starts with your commitments. Everything that has to be done, is done – that's it! The time required should be calculated as accurately as possible.

After that, you have time left over to work towards what you really want. We will deal with planning this time in the next chapter by defining your desired goals. It becomes clear that the time most people have to work on their dreams and desires is actually rather limited – at least in the beginning.

An extreme example: Person A sleeps 10 hours and works 8 hours. Including 1 hour to and from work, there are only 5 hours left to organize the day according to his own will. Over the course of the day, 1 hour is spent on eating and half an hour on household chores. That leaves only 3.5 hours.

> ➤ *Do you really want to be person A?*

A positive counterexample: Person B sleeps 6 hours. But she otherwise has the same daily routine. The fact is that by sleeping 4 hours less, she has 4 hours more time to work on her dreams and desires. She works on improving her professional situation, which will allow her to earn more and work less in 2 years. She shortens her daily work hours to 6 and allows herself an extra hour of daily sleep as a reward for the intense period. In total, she now has 6.5 hours more of life than person A.

> ➤ *If you want to be Person B, then you've gotten the gist of this book so far, and you'll be fighting for every spare hour in your daily life or goal planning.*

Final task

Start planning your own goals! Based on what you've learned in this chapter, start by making a list of your commitments. Take stock of how you would prefer to manage your commitments in order to use the time and financial resources given to you as efficiently as possible. In the following steps and chapters, this goal planning will of course be supplemented by your desired goals. As you can see in the instructions for the task, you can already start thinking about long-term goals. For now, however, the focus is on planning your commitments. First and foremost, define the following things precisely in terms of time and financial expenditure:

> ➤ Work
> ➤ Household duties

> ➤ Possibly family duties
> ➤ Cooking or eating
> ➤ Hygiene
> ➤ Sleep
> ➤ Relaxation and deceleration (e.g., lazing around, reading, massages, hobbies)
> ➤ (other) living expenses; separated by individual items such as rent, insurance, etc.

Which of these things do you need to include in your planning, and how much time and money do they cost? What do you plan to change based on the advice in this guide? (e.g., cutting back on sleep time, cooking more fresh food). Determining and planning these commitments in your daily life creates the framework for you to work on your desired goals in the next chapter and, for example, initiate long-term-changes.

Instructions for performing the task

Hanna works 8 hours a day, 6 days a week. Apart from that, she sleeps an average of 9 hours a day. She needs about 10 hours a week for the household. Cooking for herself and her family takes 2 hours a day. On the side, Hanna takes the children to school before work, which takes half an hour daily (from Monday to Friday). The weekly hygiene takes about 6 hours of her time. She earns 1,700 euros net per month. After expenses for rent including utilities, groceries and a few things for the kids, that leaves 300 euros a month to save. The spouse Jonas can contribute 200 euros per month, the rest of the money he spends on his hobbies and his share of food and rent. Most of the time Hanna and Jonas spend the rest of the money on vacations, trips or clothes because there are no other plans for it. Sometimes Hanna is dissatisfied in her life because she has no hobby to pursue. Until now, there was a lack of time – at least that was the thought. Now she wants to reschedule so that she no longer spends everything on consumption, but perhaps finances a property. She would like to involve Jonas more in the household and thus gain time. In addition, a somewhat shorter sleep duration is the goal. And maybe there is still a retirement plan in it. After all, the finances don't look that bad.

The **new** *planning in terms of the task proceeds as follows:*

Activity	Time spent per week (in hours)	Financial return per month	Financial expenditure per month
Work	48	1.700 euros net	–
Child benefit (2 children)		400 euros net	
contributed by spouse	–	200 euros	–
Household duties	7		
Cooking	14		
Take children to school	2,5		
Hygiene	6		

Sleep	49		
Real estate financing (incl. ancillary costs) instead of renting	-	-	1.000 euros
Food and other private expenses	-	-	900 euros
Retirement provision	-	-	100 euros
Total	**126,5**	**2.300 euros net**	**2.000 euros**

From the current planning it follows that from 168 hours in the week, 41.5 hours are still free after deducting the scheduled 126.5 hours. This corresponds to almost 6 hours per day! Based on her financial and time possibilities, Hanna sets herself the goal of saving her remaining 300 euros per month in order to be able to finance her own property soon. She discusses the matter with Jonas, who agrees to contribute his 200 euros as well, and is enthusiastic about the idea of financing a property. Since, with real estate financing, the rent payments would be void, despite the investment of the saved 500 euros, money would still remain, so that it would be economically intelligent planning. In 2 to 3 decades – so the long-term realistic plan – the real estate would be paid off and there would be no more financial burdens in rent or credit rates. In parallel, a supplementary private pension plan is to be taken out for around 100 euros a month. Hanna also plans to involve her spouse more in the household than before. The spouse agrees to the plan. This will give Hanna time for a hobby or certain relaxation practices. The next chapter continues with more detailed planning of hobbies and wishes.

Step 2 | What do you want?

Once your commitments are recorded, the program is complete for now. But keep the list from the final task anyway because you will still be working on it as we go along. This is your 1st list of commitments from which we determine the subsequent steps. Starting in this chapter, with step 2 – establishing your wishes and dreams.

If life were only about what has to be done and didn't correspond with your dreams at all, it would likely be quite unbearable for many people. Successful people emphasize time and again how important it is to be enthusiastic about your path. Sleeping, working and eating, are activities that serve to solve problems. People sleep so they can relax and recharge their batteries, otherwise they'd be tired and incapable of functioning properly. Work serves to solve the problem of financing your life while giving you a role in society. And eating and drinking serve to solve the problem of energy needs and sustenance in order to perform and survive.

Out of problems, and forwards to your dream world – that is the motto of this second step! Get inspired, try things out and find your passions. Make real what you have been dreaming about for a long time. And here comes the juicy bit: the easiest way to make your dreams come true is to apply the consistent planning that you have already begun to learn about. It isn't for nothing that there are training plans in the gym, dances with simple steps for the beginner in dancing, ranking with belts in martial arts, a clear sequence of teaching contents in language learning, a certain sequence of skills that are learned one after the other in pottery.

Start planning your desired goals as accurately as you learn to do certain activities in textbooks or courses. This will help you implement your desired program more consistently and acquire skills more quickly. Every now and then, people quickly lose interest when they try new things. Possible reasons are that things don't suit them or that there are obstacles that crop up. You can counteract this by planning thoroughly. This chapter tells you how to do this. In this way, you will have a high probability that your attempts at new hobbies and interests will be successful first time around.

Let yourself be inspired!

What needs the goals should satisfy

There are certain completely natural needs that humans being have. Consequently, it is appropriate to integrate them into your planning process. Please do not misunderstand this chapter, while it introduces you to those needs in detail, the goal is not to prescribe them to you. Of course, you alone decide what to put on your wish list. The following serves solely to open your eyes, so as to prevent you from disregarding these needs, that could result in you becoming dissatisfied and ultimately failing to achieve your goals, despite having done some excellent planning.

There was a phase in my life when I was on a good path, and I was experiencing professional success. I had given up my teaching job and was working in online marketing. While at the same time I started a degree program, which I successfully completed. I had regained my old discipline and increased it. Consistent goal setting was a matter of course, and achieving my goals worked like clockwork. But I overlooked one important component in all of this: my fellow human beings. With increasing success, I became so ambitious that I planned every aspect of my life in minute detail, depriving myself of any spontaneity. Social contacts didn't even happen by chance anymore. I had no fixed time scheduled for socializing, nor did I have any spontaneous time available for it. Eventually I became tired of realizing of my goals, and dissatisfaction arose in me. It was no wonder, because I had been distancing myself socially for over half a year ... until I was almost living for myself, alone in my own hyper-disciplined world. I allowed myself a few hours of free time every day, but the problem did not solve itself, as I slowly despaired. What could it be that made me feel so demotivated and powerless? I learned the reason when I received a surprise visit from 2 old friends. During their regular visits over the course of 2 weeks (they were on vacation in my area and often imposed themselves on me, which is why we met frequently), I regained more zest for life and motivation. All this time I had overlooked a central need in my planning: Man is a social being.

Because we are social creatures, the recommendation at this point is that you give enough space to social needs in your list of desired goals. How much you plan for this in your everyday life should depend on how much contact with other people you already have through your commitments (e.g., work and family). If you interact with people frequently at work and your colleagues appeal to you, you can take more space for your free time. Family and friends still have a high value and should not be neglected.

Social goals and their importance

If it's up to needs researchers, then social goals must play a central role. Companies know the same thing, which brings us back to the entrepreneurial aspect of goal planning. Companies set their goals not only in terms of orders, production, sales figures and expansion. In recent decades, corporate social responsibility (CSR) has increasingly come to the fore. This expresses a company's responsibility in the social sphere: companies are obligated to create a pleasant working environment for their employees, taking their needs into account. And indeed – even in the supposedly capitalistic and profit-oriented companies – there are abundant traits of humanity nowadays. Based on models, man is seen as a pool of skills and abilities. Accordingly, he should be enabled to develop further and realize himself.

Figure 1: Maslow's pyramid of needs

Maslow's pyramid of needs is a prime example of the position of social needs in a person's life. It is used in business administration but is equally important for every private person when setting goals and planning their own life. The pyramid has 5 levels. On the 3rd level from the bottom comes social needs. This means having certain contacts and being able to talk to them. One level above, on level 4, is the need for social respect and esteem. In other words, a distinction can be made between the need to talk to people and the need to be respected and valued by them.

In fact, the second is especially important: Who, if not the people around you, could effectively convey a feeling of respect and appreciation to you? You yourself, of course. But if you consider that doubts arise in everyone from time to time, it is good to be able to rely on people in your environment to talk you out of them. In this way, you gain confidence in difficult phases and are stronger than if you were on your own. Wolfgang Schmidbauer (2012) finely formulates this important aspect:

"Man is indeed a vertebrate in his physique, to which bones and ligaments give a firm structure. But psychologically he resembles insects, whose bodies are soft on the inside and at the same time supported and protected against the environment by an outer shell. We are psychologically dependent on being strengthened from the outside. Without symbolic confirmation or confirmation rooted in interpersonal contact, we lose our inner support."

This explanation gives you an indication as to which direction social goals should take: Ideally, you build an environment in which you make each other strong. This mutual strengthening does not have to be based exclusively on praising each other. In addition to words of praise, the focus could be on raising proportionate justified criticism and presenting it constructively.

Make new contacts and deal with people properly

You may be shy and have a small circle of friends. Or you may be so outwardly focused that you have created a large circle of friends. The important thing is not the size, but the quality of it. Meaning the feeling you have when meeting the people around you: Do you feel good around these people or not? If yes, then you have a good environment. If not, there is room for improvement. So, you could set yourself a goal to work on improving your circle of friends. Giving you the opportunity to deepen existing relationships and to look for new friends too.

Try to create a sense of reciprocity in everything positive you receive: if a person compliments you frequently, look for the person's qualities and give him or her legitimate compliments as well. If a family member always stands by you, you stand by that person too with everything you can muster. In a healthy environment, it is important not only to take, but also to give. That way, your positive relationships are likely to last longer.

What is wholly undesirable is frequent grumbling, comparison with others, competitiveness among friends or family members, frequent lying, and so on. Of course, there are exceptions. Every once in a while, competition among friends is beneficial, such as when it pushes both people towards improvement and is done fairly. Great rivals have turned into great friends in this world. It can also be normal to have no time for friends when you are busy improving other aspects of life. But apart from those few exceptions, the thoughts and actions listed at the beginning of this paragraph are generally not helpful.

I once moved in a circle of friends that was counterproductive to my happiness. If I am not to point the finger, I'd say simply that that group of people did not fit my character. One of my best friends always steered the conversation towards his professional field. And if you took the bait, he used it as an opportunity to belittle you. Another friend came from a different culture. This is an interesting thing in itself but can be a problem if he puts his culture above everything. Accordingly, he presented himself as limited and maladjusted in his views on various topics, which was a problem in that he spoke disparagingly about the female gender and belittled my views. In the family, on the other hand, I had a radical pessimist with whom I had a lot of contact: my father. As long as I did not change anything in this circle of family and friends, I always had problems: I didn't feel valued. I didn't experience support in my goals. When I addressed these issues and wanted to find solutions, none of the people concerned showed any insight. I became more and more dissatisfied as a result. Ultimately, reducing my contact with these people and even cutting it off completely in some cases helped me. I took more time making new contacts and made sure that there were similarities in character or at least openness to talk about differing points of view.

Task 1

It is normal not to get along with certain people for various reasons. Write down all the people in your circle of acquaintances, friends and family, one below the other, on a sheet of paper in the left column. For each person, think for 5 minutes about how you feel after having contact with them. In the right column, on the line corresponding to each name from the left column, record on a scale of 1 to 10 how you felt after meeting that person. With "10" meaning you feel absolutely great. Any person who receives less than a "5" leaves you feeling uncomfortable for some reason. Think about what this might be and how it threatens your goals and psychological well-being. Based on this assessment, determine the right actions to take:

➤ With which people do you engage in an open conversation that reduces problems in your interpersonal interaction?

➤ What can you do to help create a better feeling with that person in your conversations and meetings with them?

➤ With which people should you possibly break off contact? Is it worthwhile making new contacts?

➤ What social goals do you have and what people contribute to you achieving them?

Can social needs be unimportant?

I have already given an example of my own personal experiences highlighting the difficulties I had with social contacts. While I find it hard to imagine that it is different for other people, my own ideas naturally do not lend sufficient foundation to the argumentation in this book. Therefore, based on further experience and scientific research, we explore the question: *Can social needs really be unimportant?*

For you, clarification of this question is especially important if you doubt the previous explanations about the importance of social goals. Accordingly, you might also ask yourself: *"Why should*

I set myself any social goals with the help of this guidebook, when I don't care about my environment? I'm just going to do my thing, aren't I?"

Some people have this way of thinking. I also had it. It led me into misfortune, as I already explained. If we go by the findings of psychologists, sociologists and other scientists, a similar verdict emerges – social needs are important for human beings. Or going further – they increase the prospects of a healthy life. Too much loneliness makes people ill, according to an article in *TAGESSPIEGEL*. A distinction can be made between emotional and social loneliness. The former occurs when one does not have a steady partner and thus no close reference person. Social loneliness, on the other hand, affects those who are completely alone and have no contacts at all. Both forms of loneliness cannot be generalized because of people's individual reactions. But the fact of the matter is that whether it is emotional or social loneliness, it can lead to psychological problems, and even physical ailments. For example, the article in *TAGESSPIEGEL* goes on to report, citing research results from the University of Chicago, that when a person is rejected by others, the same regions in the brain react as they do to physical pain.

But what does loneliness mean? At what level of rejection, and other forms of lack of contact with people really constitutes loneliness?

Kim Bartholomew's attachment theory offers an answer. According to this theory, there are 4 different types of attachment:

1. Secure type: develops fulfilling relationships quickly and does not worry about being alone.
2. Anxious type: afraid of the possible negative consequences of social contact and risks little, although

this usually leaves him lonely and feeling exactly what he fears.

3. Possessive type: close connections to fellow human beings are his goal, which is why he already reacts very sensitively to minor rejections.

4. Rejecting type: does not want to be dependent on others, nor does he want others to be dependent on him, which is why he enters into few relationships.

Admittedly, this classification into types is very simplistic. However, you can get some helpful information from it. On the one hand, the types reveal some advantages and disadvantages of loneliness; for example, the lack of dependence can be seen as an advantage. For another, the types impressively show that there is no one form of loneliness. Considering the fact that many more attachment types could be found, loneliness has to be considered in a differentiated way.

Task 2

This task serves to clarify a question: Do you feel lonely? When you set your social goals, you should clarify this question. What counts in the assessment is purely your emotional state. Because what you feel, reflects your social satisfaction, or shows a present dissatisfaction. Therefore, keep a diary for 2 weeks starting today and question various situations in your everyday life with each entry (at least 2 entries a day). Did you feel lonely? If so, when was it and why did you feel lonely? Even with small signs of loneliness, you should make an effort to look for solutions following this task. Set a goal that fits your problem. Examples:

Go out more often with existing friends, join a club, or find new friends.

A small hint with reference to the first task: Loneliness can also stem from the fact that you do not have people in your environment who can understand certain emotional states and give you the wrong support. Therefore, when setting your social goals, try to analyze your needs carefully.

Example

A fitting example of this is therapy groups: Even the best circle of friends cannot always give the right advice to a person addicted to cocaine, a dry alcoholic, or a rape victim. After all, you have to have experienced some problems yourself in order to be able to empathize with an affected person and give good advice. Therefore, look for special interlocutors for special concerns. This radical example can also be applied to smaller issues. For example, there may be circles of friends who do not share your enthusiasm for a small hobby. So, try to find social contacts unique to your hobby. There is certainly a suitable Facebook group for every hobby, no matter how small, where you can find like-minded people and exchange ideas about your passion.

At the end of the day, this is exactly what it means to consider one's social needs in goal setting and to build a good environment for oneself: **Matching your own interests, goals, and activities – no matter how small they may be – to an appropriate set of understanding interlocutors!** In this way you learn as much as possible and can reach your goals better. After all, people should be there to help you. Finally, it should be mentioned that you can of course do certain activities all by yourself and keep the enthusiasm anyway. Time for yourself should be available on any given day anyway. A good balance between contact and alone time is optimal. You find this balance for yourself by trying things out. Just remember that being completely alone is never good in the long run, according to scientific findings.

Find desire goals

Now let's move on to defining your desired goals. First of all, it is important to distinguish between the terms: For this guide, desired goals are defined as everything that you do because you want to do it. These can be individual activities (e.g., hobbies, meeting friends) or long-term professional and private goals (e.g., new job, owning a home instead of renting). It is anything you do outside of your commitments. Commitments were the main topic in the last chapter. The main topic of this chapter is *desire goals*. These goals are closely related to your social goals because in your personal life, unlike at work, you have the freedom to create your social environment. So, try to set your desire goals based on the first 2 tasks in this chapter and matching the findings from them. In this way, you will balance 2 important components of your personal life – social and activities. You'll be able to balance any social deficits from your must-do goals (e.g., if you're rarely around people at work) with your desire goals.

There are a number of desired destinations open to you, from a wide variety of fields:

> ➢ Sports (including team sports, martial arts, athletics, gymnastics, fitness, jogging).
> ➢ Art (including pottery, sculpting, painting).

- ➢ Dance (including hip-hop, couple dance, group performances, ballet).
- ➢ Nature (including gardening, involvement in a nature conservation club, hiking, biking).

These areas, which are still quite hobby-oriented, are supplemented by others that can serve specific purposes. Should you have the desire to practice a different job in the long term, then there are still desire goals in the field of education: courses, areas of study, training etc. Sometimes just learning a new language is enough to get better prospects and a better salary in your current job.

Example

The mother of a good friend has been an outpatient caregiver for over 30 years. She goes from house to house caring for patients who need it. She is an employee for the German Red Cross. Advancement prospects are definitely there, they always have been. The catch: the friend's mother is an immigrant and although she learned the German language relatively quickly, she makes mistakes now and then in minor grammar. Additionally, because she speaks with a slight accent, she feels ashamed. The fact is that this would not stand in her way one bit and promotions have been suggested to her several times. But she refused, because it would be embarrassing for her to make mistakes when writing texts in a higher position. Now she is about to retire. She loved her job because she could help people. But she regrets not having taken advantage of the opportunities offered to incorporate her own ideas and visions into the company, and not having been able to finance a better way of life.

In this case, it would have helped to attend a German course. Maybe it wouldn't even have had to be a course, but even just a simple app on her smartphone to improve her language skills. Come to think of it, even that might not have been necessary. She had the promotions assured anyway because offers were forthcoming. Shame and fear stood in her way, in this case, irrational shame and fear.

If you are unsure what your desired goals are, then the best thing to do is to start informing yourself. The more trade magazines you read, documentaries you watch, hobbies or further education you test (there are always free test phases), and the more you are always on the lookout for something new, the sooner and faster you will find something suitable for you.

What could be the reason why you can't think of any desired goals? One possible scenario is that you are already satisfied with your life. Another possible scenario is the lack of a concrete idea: Maybe you lack a positive vision of your future life because you have been trapped in your personal hamster wheel for too long. You may be afraid to take responsibility for yourself and to set your sights on your goals. Another conceivable cause is the classic problem of the digital age: You have too many ideas and set yourself too many goals at the same time.

If you are currently satisfied with your life, look for small areas of improvement. If you don't find any, then you probably already have the right "must" and "want" goals. This means that you can use the advice in the other chapters of this book to optimize your planning, but otherwise leave everything as it is.

The situation is different if you are dissatisfied with your life:

➢ Do you regularly miss your goals?

➢ Your everyday life is too much of a burden for you?

➢ Your job, your free time, and the people around you leave you with too many negative emotions?

➢ You lack ideas for creative pass-times, and it seems like you are wasting your life?

Exactly for these problems the following contents have been designed to inspire you, to point out your talents, and to provide you with concrete instructions on how to choose suitable desired goals.

Example

U.S. actor Denzel Washington, known as a unique character actor, and for his involvements outside of acting, spoke several times to college graduates. His motivational speeches are listed on several YouTube channels in a row with those of the greatest entrepreneurs and politicians out there. In one of his speeches, he made a very important point: He said that *what matters to* us as human beings is *not* always how *much* we have, but *what* we have. However, it is more important to do what you love in life and what is right for you. By following your passions and building on what you already have – whether it's character traits like patience or resources like money – you increase your chance of success.

Be inspired and courageously try new things

Often people do not follow their desired goals because there is some uncertainty or improbability associated with it. From this we can infer the central advantage that commitments have: Living the life one has to live – working, sleeping, feeding oneself, taking care of the household, taking care of one's health – is associated with security and normality. One does not step out of line. Accordingly, you rarely have to explain yourself to people. If you are puzzled at this point, the following example will explain what is meant: Imagine you are observing 2 people. One person works 8 hours a day, then goes home and makes his dinner. The rest of the time is spent watching series on the couch. The other person works 8 hours, also has a mini-job and is doing distance learning in parallel. She is often exhausted because she manages a heavy workload. That's why she uses Sundays for extensive relaxation. With which of these people would you be more likely to object to the daily routine? Usually, it's the second person who has 2 jobs and is studying at the same time. Because having such a workload, seems abnormal.

But since when is not normal automatically bad? As long as you feel that your regeneration is sufficient and you make good use of the small time-outs during the day, you can have a busy schedule and still be satisfied and recovered. If you want to find your true desired goals and make maximum efficient use of your lifetime, please get inspired! Dare to go unfamiliar ways. Possibly this entails that you try out new things. Do not be afraid of it.

Example

On goal setting, Denzel Washington recited an anecdote in one of his speeches. He was talking about a task on an IQ test: In this test, there are 9 dots in 3 rows inside a box. The task is to draw 5 lines with a pencil without lifting the pencil. The crux: the 5 lines are supposed to connect all the 9 dots. This task can only be completed successfully if the lines are drawn to the outside of the box. With this example, Washington appeals to students to think outside the box; that is, to pursue even unusual lines of thought and act accordingly.

The desire goals are what make you leave your comfort zone. For these goals, you go the extra mile in your life. You no longer just do what you have to do, but what is close to your heart. If you want to succeed in this desire program and achieve the goals, your goals should come from your heart. Afterwards, think of these wish goals as exactly what they are: a wish planning exercise in which you are purposeful but feel no pressure. Who cares if you miss a free throw at the next handball game in one of Germany's lowest leagues? Who cares if your correspondence course goes to waste? Maybe it just wasn't the right thing for you. You still have a full-time job and all the security you need in life.

The desire goals are waiting for you. They are waiting for all your creativity, your courage, your enthusiasm, your passion, your vision, and your dreams. Do not be afraid to make mistakes! Don't think about having to justify to others why you do or don't do a certain hobby! Be open to even the most outlandish hobbies and ideas, because maybe there is just the right thing for you, hidden in one of the insane ideas!

Task 3

Start working on a preliminary list of desired goals. For this purpose, take a blank sheet of paper and write down all the goals that you would like to achieve. The exact time planning up to realization as well as the weighing up process, comes later. For now, just collect goals. When making your preliminary list, try to incorporate your findings from the social-needs tasks. Which desired goals are appropriate for meeting your social needs? Also, if you are unhappy with your full-time job, rent payments, or other obligations in your life, consider what opportunities there are to make long-term changes based on desire goals. Goals like financing a home, traveling more often, studying while working, continuing your education, and similar goals are absolutely right on the money here. More advice awaits you in the coming subchapters. Your list of desired goals may be extensive.

Personal hobbies and talents – great opportunities lie dormant here

Ever thought that hobbies and talents can become a profession? It's not the rule, but it is possible. Especially in today's times, it's easier to monetize hobbies and talents. Let's say you have handyman skills and put it on your wish list to refinish an old piece of furniture every day. You sand down an old cabinet, prime it and repaint it. You cover the inside of the cabinet with fabric. The result is a French Provence style masterpiece. As a joke, you get the idea to put the cabinet up for sale on *eBay Classifieds*. You end up making a huge profit on the sale, because people are willing to pay for unique products that exude personality. Over time, you get the idea to share your artwork on social media, create an online store with a simple modular system, and build a small business. As a sideline, you earn a high 4-digit amount per year. What's more, you're doing something that's close to your heart and that you enjoy. You receive recognition via social media. This also satisfies your social needs.

Hobby and talent = profession

This simple formula can work if you want it to. If you find it too stressful and would rather let your hobby, be a hobby, you are of course equally free to do so. Whether as a profession or for fun, promote hobbies and talents anyway! Do more of what you enjoy. Develop your talents. Work to perhaps turn your hobby into a profession. Not only hobbies and talents are important: expanding your knowledge and interests also make excellent additions to your list. These tips will help you find and set appropriate desired goals.

Notice

Practicing hobbies should never become stressful. Otherwise, they end up not serving as relaxation and filling you less and less with joy. Ideally, objectives concerning your hobbies should be formulated as loosely as possible. Leave room for spontaneity. As soon as you notice that the hobby is stressing you out in some way, or that it is taking up too much of your time so that you can hardly relax during the day, you should tone down your goals.

"One day your time will come. At your deathbed will be not only friends and family, but also the other companions of your life: your talents and abilities. They will tell you that it is a pity that you left them unused. It was clear from the beginning that you would eventually pass away. The talents,

however, could have outlived you. Now, unfortunately, they will be buried along with you." – Denzel Washington (U.S. actor)

With this quote we conclude the statements of Denzel Washington. With this sentence, the actor encouraged students to use their talents and abilities as well as possible. Mistakes are all too normal in the process. Even big mistakes can happen. But what matters in life is to have the courage to make mistakes. And when you fall, always fall forward, and keep going. Just don't fall back ...

Turning old into new – skills over time

In your search for desired goals for comprehensive goal planning, one last piece of advice awaits you: never get into the habit of definitively writing off a goal based on past experiences. If you couldn't do something in the past or were talked out of it, it doesn't necessarily have to be wrong for you today. Over the years, many things may have changed in the way you think and act. It may be that activities that were unsuitable for you 5 to 10 years ago suit you today.

Author Bernhard Moestl also addresses this issue in his bestseller *Der Weg des Tigers* (2013). He cites an experience from his own life: He was repeatedly told in his environment that he had no manual skills. What's more, he didn't enjoy doing manual work. He therefore often let other people go ahead with the work in question. He was convinced of his own inability. One day he found himself in a situation where he was forced to renovate a photo studio. Helpers were not available. The hardship of the situation led him to try himself. He took it upon himself to forget his perceived years of incompetence and take on the task with an open mind. The result: all the renovations looked perfectly satisfactory. Apparently, he didn't have 2 left hands after all.

What Moestl wants to say with this example, and what he comes directly to later, is the fact that in the course of time every human being undergoes further development. Why should the human being not learn new abilities in the context of further development? Quote from Moestl: *"But it is a fact that we learn and develop further. And that today we might be able to do things with ease that would have been impossible for us 10 years ago."*

This state of affairs can be explained transparently in 2 words: **Transfer benefits**. If you learn certain things or activities in the course of your life, you also benefit from them in relation to other activities. For example, a person who can already play 10 instruments can learn each additional instrument with less effort than a person who does not yet play any instruments. In addition, there is another phenomenon that is unfortunately little researched scientifically: if you have tried an activity for a while and then take a longer break (whether years, months, weeks), you can learn the activity more easily after the break. Some learning concepts make use of this, pointing to long-term memory: if you cram through an activity at all costs, you will only retain the sequences in short-term memory and have a harder time recalling them. In contrast, people who deal with the content regularly are able to store it in long-term memory, from where it is easier to recall once it sits.

Task 4

Transfer these insights to your desired goals by thinking about whether there are things you would like to do but are doubting your abilities. Think back to your childhood: was there anything there, in your youth, or in your young adult life that you very much wanted to do, but for a variety of reasons it didn't work out? If so, write it down on a blank piece of paper. Then, for each of these things, think about why you didn't master it or couldn't make it work. Then answer the question of whether it could be different today. It is best to try out the activities without obligation. This is the best way to find out whether an activity that didn't suit you in the past suits you better today. If so, add it to your preliminary list of desired goals.

From mere goal to action

How many desired goals do you have now? What comes into question for you? In what do you want to rediscover yourself? If you have formulated some wish goals with the help of the previous tasks and contents in this chapter, the question now arises as to how to operationalize them:

How do you translate your wishes and dreams into actions? How many wish-goals can, or should you set at the same time in order not to overwhelm yourself in view of the parallel existing obligations?

It's a little easier with your day-to-day responsibilities. For example, a certain amount of time is usually set aside for your work. Your superiors or the boss take over the task allocation directly. Household chores, on the other hand, can be planned flexibly and are usually done when there is time – or they are not done at all ... Nevertheless, chores usually require a little less planning than voluntary goals.

When it comes to your desired goals, you are the boss: you determine which goal you choose, how you divide it into intermediate steps, and finally, how you achieve it. You also determine the quantity of goals. You are responsible for your goals. Of course, as many people do, you can prefer to listen to other people's advice and follow their wishes in your life. Or you can do nothing at all. Then you have no responsibility and don't have to plan anything. But then this advice has done nothing. It's time to act and tackle your dreams. For this, it is essential that you take responsibility for your goal setting and actions.

It's time to take responsibility

If you've been reluctant to take responsibility for your actions, now is the time to rethink. You are faced with several options for dealing with the effect your environment has on you. In all the options for goal setting that you have gathered from the first 2 steps of this guide, the environment will play a role. The reason for this is that pretty much every goal involves other people. Even if you keep something like a diet to yourself, sooner or later friends, family or co-workers will notice that something has changed in your eating habits. For some it will be a reason for praise, but for others it will be a reason for blame.

Example

You shouldn't always take praise and criticism seriously these days. An amazing example is the reactions to an Instagram post by plus-size model Ashley Graham. The woman has her curves and medically she is overweight, but she accepts it. She is happy with it and works successfully as a model. An extensive fan base admires her. So far, everything is fine. Now Ashley Graham has apparently nevertheless sporty hobbies. Practicing sports, but still staying true to her overweight figure and being happy with it, do not contradict each other. Nevertheless, when she posted a photo of herself at the gym, she gathered plenty of criticism from her followers. She no longer remains true to herself and does not stand by her body it was said sporadically. This form of criticism is inappropriate.

This example is not intended to start a debate about the justification of sports, obesity, or physical ideals. It is only meant to illustrate that nowadays people are sometimes so strongly focused on one point of view that they can no longer differentiate. So, it can happen that even with – from your point of view – highly praiseworthy goals you get to hear a lot of criticism. Be prepared to hear perhaps the strangest and most absurd criticism of your decisions. After all, the philosophy of the critics in the example would mean that no overweight person can be proud of his figure if he practices sports. But doesn't every person have the right to practice sports hobbies in public?

There will always be criticism. It helps to listen to this criticism. The more meaningful the criticism seems from your point of view, the more it may be included in the decision about setting and pursuing goals. But the decision is always yours or yours and the other people involved. Negative circumstances in the environment may arise sooner or later. You decide whether you want to complain and pass on the responsibility for the decision or whether you want to live your dream life on your own initiative despite the unavoidable resistance. As soon as you realize your personal responsibility and act accordingly, you will realize that you have the ability to influence and control your environment and decide how far you will let *it* influence *you*.

Refine your list of desired goals

When making your list of desired goals, it is first and foremost important that you write down what is realistic and plannable from your current point of view. It doesn't matter whether the goal is short, medium or long-term. After all, you divide the goals into intermediate steps for better operationalization anyway. More about this awaits you in the 4 steps of this book, when you precisely formulate your long-term planning.

Estimate time required

After formulating realistic goals, you need to find out how much time is behind your desired goals. This is the only way to choose the right amount of goals to pursue at the same time, so as not to overburden yourself. If you choose too many desired goals in addition to your commitments, you run risks. On the one hand, it is possible that due to the large number of goals, none of them will be implemented properly and the commitments will suffer. On the other hand, it can happen that you pursue all goals well for a while, but then you are too busy and mental and physical fatigue sets in, which completely slows you down.

Therefore, the next step after writing down your desired goals is to estimate the time required for each of them. It can be the daily time spent, but it can also be the time spent over a longer time horizon. For example, when traveling, it's hard to measure daily time because you don't travel every day. Here, it makes more sense to report the monthly time spent.

Important: Estimate the time required realistically and generously. This also includes preparatory measures, such as packing the sports bag or shopping in advance for an excursion with the family (e.g., provisions and tent for a camping weekend). If you want more general knowledge and use your smartphone as a knowledge library for that, there's no need for preparatory measures. Regular trips to the library, on the other hand, require preparatory measures. Nevertheless, there are also goals that do not require additional time, such as quitting smoking. If anything, they give you more time because you no longer have to buy cigarettes. In your list next to each goal, note how much extra time it will cost you.

Final task

Revise the list you have worked with so far in the 4 tasks of the chapter. You have written down desired goals. Now cross off the desired goals from the list that do not fully convince you. Also, cross off the goals that don't seem realistic at all from today's point of view. It doesn't have to be a "goodbye", because maybe the goals will become realistic in a few years or months. For now, however, they are not and do not belong on the list. Next to each remaining desired goal, enter numbers that describe its priority. The number "1" represents the highest priority, "5" represents the lowest priority. Also, write down the amount of time you expect to spend on each goal. The quantity of your goals does not matter at first.

Instructions for performing the task

Let's take Ingo as an example, who, while reading this chapter, identified the following desired goals for himself in the individual tasks:

- ➤ In tasks 1 and 2, he has none because he is very satisfied with his social environment.
- ➤ In Task 3, he has entered as goals a better salary at his full-time job, which he intends to achieve through further training and the associated acquisition of new qualifications. In addition, in Task 3 he has formulated the goal of resuming playing table tennis in the club. In fact, he quite misses this passion from his youth.
- ➤ Task 4 brought Ingo to the realization that he had always been told that he couldn't cook. The origin of this claim is quite ridiculous because he has only once failed to cook a dish; stupidly when he cooked for his entire circle of acquaintances. Accordingly, the mishap had great repercussions. Because Ingo has a lot of time, especially on weekends and sometimes in the evenings, he takes it upon himself to try cooking every now and then. This way he can possibly give his wife a nice surprise.

Ingo sets the priority numbers for his desired goals as follows:

- ➤ Advanced training: 1
- ➤ Table tennis: 2
- ➤ Cooking: 4

Obviously, improving his professional situation is most important to him, but taking up his old hobby is almost as important. Lastly, in Ingo's eyes, cooking is more of a nice add-on that he passes the time with when everything else is going well and he has a lot of available free time for it. Therefore, cooking has a lower priority. Based on the priority numbers, he determines the amount of time that is highest in training. He sticks to the curriculum: His advanced training should take a year and a half in total, with a recommended learning time of 20 hours a week. To be on the safe side, he adds 5 hours, most of which he spends on weekends off. Table tennis is scheduled twice a week, for a total of 1.5 hours per training session, so that 3 hours a week are spent on it. But wait: You surely remember that preparatory measures should also be included in a time planning. For Ingo, this means that for 3 hours of table tennis per week, one and 1.5 hours of preparatory measures (packing a bag, traveling there and back) have to be added. So, it costs him 4.5 hours of time per week. Cooking is less important. For Ingo, it would already be enough if he could find 3 hours on each of 2 weekends a month to cook 1 or 2 dishes; so, we are at an estimated monthly time expenditure of 6 hours.

This information is not yet binding. But they already give a direction as to what is important to Ingo and how much time is required. This will enable him to refine his objectives in the following steps or chapters of the guidebook and ultimately draw up a precise overall plan for his goals.

Step 3 | Filter and decide – what will you do?

Filtering is the step that helps you figure out which of your many goals to tackle first. You have already applied 1 filter in the 1st step of goal setting: The "must" filter. These are the goals or duties you will be forced to pursue because you need them for your life. They are relevant in planning because they limit the time and energy available for your other goals.

We leave out the "must", i.e., the obligations, for the time being. We will start at the end of the 2nd step, namely with your desired goals – **List 1**. Ideally, after the last exercises, you will have a list of several goals. Great enthusiasts and visionaries may have 20 goals, modest people may have 2 or 3. The amount doesn't matter as long as everything you care about is written down.

The more goals you have, or the more time individual goals take, the sooner you will notice the dilemma that often arises for unsuccessful people without clear goal planning: The goals may collide with each other, and if you want to pursue all your desires, an enormous amount of time is required. You may not even have that much time available. Do you experience the same problem?

Whatever is on your wish list, it must not overwhelm you. Therefore, filtering becomes necessary. For this, take your list 2 with desire goals and your list 1, with obligations. Write down how much time your commitments take up each day. Normally, with a

40-to-48-hour job, you won't have more than 3 to 5 hours during the week to work on your desired goals. You realize what's coming up: filtering. How do the goals interact with each other? This is one of the questions that will be clarified in order to optimize the goal selection process.

There are several methods to help you with filtering. I have 4 methods ready for you. You don't have to use them in this order. Accordingly, you don't have to do the individual tasks in this chapter in order. It's a good idea to read through the entire chapter first and then decide which methods you want to try. This is the best way to find the right filter method for you.

Filtering method 1: Search complementary targets

From my studies I have taken the brilliant approach of subdivision and filtering according to goal relationships: Goals are in different relationships to each other; for it to help you in the implementation, already a subdivision into complementary, conflicting, and indifferent goals is sufficient. Does it all sound too scientific? No problem, let's make it easier ...

Complementary goals are compatible with each other. They support each other. By pursuing 2 goals that support each other, the achievement of 1 goal simultaneously promotes the achievement of the other goal. This is beneficial to you when it comes to pursuing more than 1 of your goals. This is because when you have 2 complementary goals, it is easier to implement. For example, for the list above, it would look like this:

> ➤ The goals of "dieting" and "exercising more" are 2 different goals but support each other.

➢ Quitting smoking and sport can also be seen as complementary, because sport distracts from the difficult smoking cessation (keyword: addiction shift), so that ideally it is carried through more consistently and successfully.

➢ Not complementary, on the other hand, would be for working people to do distance learning and weekend trips at the same time. After all, distance learning requires a large investment of time. If you don't invest part of your weekends, you'll have a hard time successfully completing your studies while working a 48-hour job at the same time.

When you set complementary goals, you have the chance to accomplish more goals from your wish list in the time you have left each day. Always make sure that you don't choose complementary goals just because they complement each other, and you can do as much as possible. They have to be really close-to your heart. So: Don't just add new goals to your list at the drop of a hat that complement the other goals! Instead, strictly follow your list of commitments and desired goals.

It is also helpful to identify **conflicting goals**, i.e., those that interfere with each other. This will give you information about which goals you should possibly not pursue at the same time. An example I just mentioned: 48-hour job as a commitment and distance learning and weekend getaways as a desired goal. In rare cases, this approach can work, but in a full-time job with working hours on Saturdays, weekend trips and distance learning are conflicting, because both eat up a lot of the remaining time.

The **indifferent goals** are those that do not influence each other. After knowing about complementary, conflicting, and indifferent goals, it suggests itself that you prefer the complementary goals in your plans, because this way you can work off your desire goals best. If you are particularly concerned about a goal that is difficult to reconcile with the other goals, then you should think carefully about whether this goal is really worth giving up all the other desired goals for, or vice versa and then think about which ones could be better out off for a later point in time.

Task 1

Look at your lists of commitments and desired goals. Consider what relationships emerge among the goals. On a separate sheet of paper, write down which goals are complementary, conflicting, and indifferent to each other. Since you have to meet your commitments anyway, ideally you will start from this and determine which desire goals are most compatible with your commitments: Which desire goals are complementary to your commitments? Which desired goals are more likely to conflict and should be avoided for the time being?

Filtering method 2: Match targets to character

Every person is unique. Individual characters entail individual goals. That's why you're reading this book – your individual and external advice hasn't satisfied you yet. Now you are looking for answers within yourself. In view of this, there is hardly anything better than to think a few basic thoughts about who you really are in the first place ...

Sometimes the answer to this question is easier than the answer to the question of what you want to do. Do you perhaps manage to categorize yourself right off the bat, for example, as a family person, a career person, a sports fanatic, a social person? Of course, in a way, that's pigeonholing, which is simplistic, and maybe you don't want to categorize yourself that way. However, sometimes simple pigeonholing gets you further than complicated thinking.

Example

If you enjoy being around people frequently and can think of few things better than spending your time with friends and family, then it suggests that you have a strong social streak that you could further promote with your goals. Or maybe you are the complete opposite of a social person? Do you have a specific passion (e.g., music, art, sports, IT, gaming, technical literature) and set a career path in mind where relationships play little role for you? In this case, it would be a good idea to take a path in which you promote your skills straight away. You are a career person with high ambitions.

A character cannot always be classified as simplistically as in these 2 examples. And yet, pigeonholing is useful now and then. Because if you have no ideas at all about which goals from the list best suit you, and balance is already assured, you simply choose the simple way of pigeonholing: characterize yourself with one word, choose the most appropriate goal, and try it out to see if it suits you.

However, there are characters who are particularly complicated and for whom pigeonholing cannot be applied.

Perhaps you know it yourself from your own life: You are torn between 2 things. On the one hand, you want nothing more than to work in your dream career, but on the other hand, you care a lot about your family. What now? Which goals should you choose? If you can't decide clearly, then set the goals in a balanced way. For example, your work already covers a large part of the "career" area. It would be a good idea to choose less career-oriented goals among the desire goals, but to improve your social situation instead. Adapt your goals to your current character and check regularly every few months to see if your goals still suit you. There are plenty of impressive stories of career people who thought to themselves after a few years or decades: No, this is not what I want. Their character changed or they realized that there was another side to them from the beginning. They quit their jobs and traveled the world or devoted more time to their families.

My experience

I always face enormous challenges when selecting new targets because my character is so multi-layered. No doubt this trait has various merits, but sometimes it makes things more difficult. So, it is with me for goal setting. I almost never avoid trying activities for several weeks or even months before setting goals. Adapting goals to character can be highly complex and require permanent mindfulness to make the necessary changes. What helped me were regular self-tests. There are many of these available on the internet. You can take self-tests for your job, personality, suitable hobby, family and for numerous other fields. Feel free to try out a few of them. They are especially advantageous for people who find it difficult to assess their character. They give advice on even the most contradictory character traits and the most ambivalent answers, which may be perfectly applicable.

Method 3 to filter: Favor the influenceable goals

You know when you've got it all figured out and planned great, but success also depends on other people who are just unreliable? Most of the time in studies, school, work, and team sports – everywhere there are dependencies – there is this one group partner who ruins all the work. It can be the same with goals. Because some goals can't be influenced just by you.

The model *Three Circles of Influence* according to Stephen R. Covey provides a better understanding. It divides the goals into 3 spheres of influence:

➢ controllable by me alone
➢ Influenceable by me
➢ concerns me

If a goal is **controllable by you alone,** then you can work on it and don't have to consult with anyone in your approach. According to Covey, these are the goals you should prefer. The central advantage is absolute sovereignty, the central disadvantage is absolute responsibility. Regarding responsibility, this guidebook has already given 1 or 2 important pieces of advice: Even though it is cited by Covey as a disadvantage, it still comes with many advantages. Because if you take responsibility, you are also in control. That's exactly why you are absolutely independent with a goal that is controllable by you alone. A perfect example can be found in Calvin Hollywood's guidebook *Who Will, Who Can!* (2018).

Example

Hollywood talks about how his son came back home after school and reported that he had detention. The reason, he said, was a fight with another boy. Hollywood's son managed to get the other boy blamed. Nevertheless, both boys got detention, which Hollywood's son thought was unfair. The father explained the problem to his son: the moment he shifted the blame to the other boy, he relinquished control of the situation and became dependent on him. If he had accepted at least part of the blame, he would have been able to argue better in front of the teachers.

Admittedly, for many individuals, responsibility is something that comes with a queasy feeling. Many individuals resist having control and responsibility over a situation. After all, this results in obligations and full liability for mistakes. The good thing is that with desire goals that are controllable by you alone, you are accountable only to yourself.

Next, there are the **goals that you can influence**: These are goals whose success you influence, but which you don't completely control. Be attentive at this point because these goals make up a large part of your life:

➢ Family decisions are goals that can be influenced by you, but not controlled by you alone.
➢ Finding a spouse is a goal that is highly dependent on another person.

> ➢ Goals for team sports or hobbies with others are ideally made with the agreement of all concerned.

> ➢ When starting a business with another person and running the business, there are all kinds of goals ahead that are not determined by you alone.

Family goals and the search for a permanent partner in particular require a great deal of consideration for others in the formulation and implementation of goals. For example, even the most charismatic and eloquent people do not necessarily find a partner for life in a hurry or within the targeted time frame. Such goals, which can be influenced by you but cannot be completely decided, should only be on your goals agenda if they are a) particularly important to you and at the same time b) complementary with other goals.

Example

Your goals are "travel" and "find friends". The former can be controlled by you alone, the latter can only be "influenced" by you. Therefore, it is best if you do not plan the second goal in a binding way but integrate it into your everyday life. Fortunately, "traveling" and "making friends" are possible complementary goals: For example, while traveling, you can try to meet people along the way. This would be a way to pursue a goal that can only be influenced without much effort.

Lastly, the **concern-me goals**: These types of goals are irrelevant because they are outside of your decision-making power. They cannot be influenced by you, or only to a limited extent. Working on these goals would be like an enormous effort that does not pay off.

Conclusion: It's all about your life and how you shape it. Get the most control over your life by choosing goals that are fully within your control. For the rare goals that require you to coordinate with other people (e.g., family, friends), make sure that you all communicate clearly and in detail with each other about how the goal is to be approached. That way, you're sure that people will go along with it. Here, once again, the system characteristics become apparent. Especially with goals that are not fully controllable by you, many unforeseen interactions can occur when pursuing goals.

Task 2

Look at your list of desired goals. Review and write down on a piece of paper which of the desired goals are controllable by you alone. Mark these goals clearly because they are to be preferred. Then write down the goals that can only be influenced by you. Ask yourself whether it is really worthwhile to plan these goals, where your success depends on other people. If they are important family goals, then write down some of these goals, of course. After all, a happy family life requires compromise in living together. Nevertheless, try to plan and choose the majority of your desired goals so that they are controllable by you alone – full responsibility, but full independence and control!

Method 4 to filter: Focus on your strengths

Focusing on your strengths will not only help you filter but may also add a few new goals to your list. You may even change your previous basic attitude with this filtering method. Because many people who don't succeed or are longing for success are characterized by the problem of focusing on their weaknesses or being blinded by their weaknesses. If you change your mindset and focus on your strengths from an optimistic point of view, you may make better progress. Various sayings from successful people go argumentatively in this direction:

- ➤ *"Those who work with their strengths become stronger."* – Ingo Krawiec
- ➤ *"Success consists in having the very skills that are in demand at the moment."* – Henry Ford
- ➤ *"One should not consider the worth of a man according to the great qualities he has, but according to the use he makes of you."* – La Rochefoucuald
- ➤ *"Think rather of what you have than of what you lack."* – Marcus Aurelius

So, what counts in life is to focus on your strengths. Why should you let your weaknesses stop you from doing something you're not good at? Maybe because others instigate you to do it. But no, that's enough! You finally take responsibility for your actions. You decide what you want to do. Your strengths should come to the fore. Promote them and – you remember the last chapter – regularly try things that you couldn't do before. Because you may have gained new skills in the meantime without knowing it.

Of course, if there's something you particularly like but haven't mastered, you may develop and learn new skills. Ideally, however, the majority of your goals should be those that are compatible with your strengths. That's the best way to move forward.

Task 3

What was your previous mindset? Have you undervalued yourself and stood in your own way because you thought too much about your weaknesses? If so, then turn the tables now: Think about what your strengths are **and** what you'd like to do. Mark each goal that meets these 2 criteria in your wish list of goals.

Final task

You now know various different methods of filtering. Finally, apply all of them, whether you have already done the 3 tasks in this chapter or not. Once you have done all 4 methods, you can do an overall evaluation, and decide on the desired goals that seem best to you at the moment, and that fit your time frame. Make sure you don't calculate too tightly and don't forget to take into account your commitments. Speaking of commitments: Now is the time when you can better make modifications in scheduling your commitments to give yourself more space. Cutting your sleep by an hour or 2 to make more time for your desired goals is worth doing now. Because now you have an overview of your desired goals and commitments – that is, your complete goal program – with the associated time commitment. Through this overview you can bring the commitments and desired goals even better and more precisely in line with each other. All desired goals that do not fit into your schedule because of the commitments, you put aside for the time being. You can schedule them for later as part of the long-term planning in the next step.

Instructions for performing the task

Theo currently has the following commitments:

➢ Sleep: around 8 hours a day so far (a bit more on weekends).

➢ Hygiene: about half an hour a day.

➢ Full-time job: 5 x 9 hours a day during the week (including 1 hour a day to and from work).

➢ take care of his children: just under 2 hours a day to take the children to school and pick them up again, as well as playing and reading to them in the evening.

➢ Preparing and eating food: sometimes the wife does it, sometimes Theo; all in all, it takes about 1.5 hours a day.

During the week, 3 hours per day remain for the pursuit of desired goals, because 21 hours already have to be factored in for obligations. On weekend days – minus the 9 hours of work and plus just under 2 additional hours of sleep – there are about 10 hours each day. So, Theo has 3 hours a day from Monday to Friday and 10 hours on Saturday and Sunday.

Additionally, as a person with an affinity for music, he has the following desired goals with an estimated time commitment:

➢ learning to dance with the wife; every Tuesday and Thursday 2 hours each (+ 0,5 hours in total for going and coming back).

➢ Learn to play the piano; 1 hour each Monday and Friday (+ 1 hour total to and from).

➢ Spend more time with friends because most of the time is spent with family; do something with friends for 5 hours on each of 2 Sunday evenings a month.

➢ Find more time for relaxation and promote well-being (e.g., through massages, wellness); book a wellness program every weekend for 3 hours and once during the week for 1 hour (+ 1 hour total to get there and back).

➢ travel around the world (only possible during vacation).

You can already tell from the goals that Theo and his family are not short of money. After all, anyone who books wellness programs twice a week, travels the world and wants to learn to dance and play the piano professionally must have quite a bit of money at their disposal. In fact, Theo and his wife are top earners.

Nevertheless, goal planning is not advantageous because, especially during the week, there is hardly any time left for anything other than the scheduled activities. Although the desired goals do not go beyond the scope of time availability, Theo knows that a tightly scheduled plan is associated with disadvantages. Even if schedules include partial hobbies, there should be plenty of free, unscheduled time in a sustainable plan. After consulting with his wife, Theo determines that learning to dance is out of the question. After all, someone has to take care of the kids, so they both can't be away at the same time. So, Theo and his wife decide to attend intensive dance classes on the 4 vacations they have together each year.

➢ Thus, "dancing" and "traveling" become complementary goals.

> On the condition that Theo gets up an hour earlier every day and looks after the children more intensively in the mornings, his wife agrees to him learning to play the piano 2 evenings a week.

> Spending more time with his friends on the weekend *and* booking wellness programs is not okay for Theo's family. Much of their time together would be lost and the wife would have to take care of the children for almost the entire weekend. That's why everyone decides by consensus that Theo will do one thing. He commits to meeting up with his friends more often. From time to time, he goes to wellness with the friends, which makes the goals "more meetings with friends" and "more wellness" complementary.

> Even doing an hour of wellness during the week is out of the question after consulting with the wife. Instead, they both decide to give each other a massage or a soothing bath every now and then in the evening. This brings them closer together physically, something that was often lacking in their marriage.

We realize that because of his family, Theo has a lot of goals that he can't control on his own. Instead, he has to discuss almost everything with his family. Nevertheless, compromises can be made in which Theo's wife has plenty of freedom and can sometimes do what she likes. The bottom line is that Theo has made some goals complementary or incorporated them into his other day-to-day obligations. It seems like little has changed in the daily routine because a lot of the desired goals have been shifted to vacation time. But meeting his friends more often and living out his musical vein – these goals, which are important to him, have been achieved. Within families, you just have to bake smaller rolls now and then.

Step 4 | Carry out long-term planning

If you set your goals for the short, medium, and long term and follow them consistently, your whole life will follow a plan. Through filtering, from the last chapter, you have decided which goals you want to tackle first. By doing this, you have chosen an order in which to address each goal. Long-term planning gives you the opportunity to also take into account the desire goals in the plans for which you currently do not have time. Because the planning is long-term and knows no restricting time horizons.

For example, you've realized that the fastest way to make changes to your full-time job is to start setting the course now. Because your full-time job is a significant part of your life, it makes sense to start planning here: What goals will help me improve my full-time job (e.g., continuing my education to increase my salary and prospects) or get a new and, in my eyes, better full-time job? (e.g., going to college, getting a different education, starting my own business).

In addition to a full-time job, long-term planning also helps you in your private life. You can plan together with your spouse when and under what conditions you would like to have a child. Example: First increase savings, create better living conditions and then plan the offspring.

Although this 4th step is mentioned in reference to "long-term planning", it also includes short-term planning. Because long-term planning definitely includes short-term plans anyway — at least if you want to be really precise and thus more likely to succeed. Long-term goals require a division into intermediate stages. These intermediate stages are again divided into smaller stages and then further subdivisions take place. Without intermediate stages, the danger that you will stray is great.

If you want to put it piquantly, but also consistently and correctly, then you come to the realization that there is basically no separate short-term planning. It does exist, but it is part of a higher-level long-term plan. Accordingly, the people most likely to achieve their goals are those who consider how to do short-term planning in conjunction with long-term goals. This gives even the smallest short-term goals an overarching larger meaning. Consequently, motivation is highest to achieve the goals.

With all that you have gathered in the previous chapters of this book – all your commitments and desired goals, your duties and dreams – you should now create a long-term plan in which one cog meshes with another and the smallest goals become long-term puzzle pieces. They become puzzle pieces of a fascinating and impressive project that every human being has to master – life.

Ranking of goals

The foundation that helps you to bring order and clarity into your planning is the division of the goals according to their ranking. This is where what, many authors in books and on websites, and numerous coaches and psychologists, suggest comes into play: the division of goals into stages. In business studies, at least 4 stages are regularly used for larger goals:

- ➤ The **overall goal** is what you want to achieve in the end.
- ➤ The **intermediate goal** is subordinate to the overall goal.
- ➤ The **subgoal** is subordinate to the intermediate goal.
- ➤ At the bottom of the chain is the **stage goal**, which is immediately tackled as a short-term goal.

Goals divided into stages keep your stamina and motivation higher. Imagine you want to lose 20 kilograms. Such a diet takes time, especially if it is to be safe from a health point of view.

Let's start from something conceivably impractical: You don't have a scale at home, and you don't weigh yourself all the time. As a result, you are in the dark and don't know what your goal is. As a result, you can't see any intermediate successes in front of you. Your stamina and motivation decrease in the face of the stresses and strains of dieting, with no certainty of whether they will pay off. Because you do not weigh yourself.

In contrast, you can now imagine a person who weighs himself every week on his diet and sees the kilos fall. He has the certainty that the diet works and can be happy about getting closer and closer to his goal.

Stages and precise summaries of intermediate steps on the way to your goal bring it to the point: your success so far, your progress, your stamina. You'll be more motivated to fight internal and external resistance and still pursue your goal. Doesn't that sound appealing?

Therefore, a ranking is established for each major goal. This ranking tells you which individual steps you need to take to achieve the goal. Here is an example of a ranking for the goal of quitting smoking. It is assumed to be a medium-term or even short-term goal (see: "Time Reference of Goals" from Step 1 of this book), because consistent smoking cessation is possible within less than 5 years.

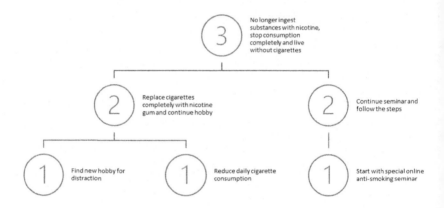

The numbers 1 represent the first short-term goals that are formulated: You start smoking cessation by consuming fewer cigarettes and taking up a hobby to shift addiction or distraction. For 2, there is the professional online seminar that gives you further advice on how to carry out the smoking cessation. After that – it can be for example after 2 months – the seminar is continued according to the instructions of the seminar leader. Meanwhile, the cigarettes are completely replaced by nicotine gum to improve the cessation process. After, for example, 8 months, the cigarettes can be completely discontinued. For the time being, weaning is then successful.

This is how a ranking works: What has to be done first and for how long? What comes next and how long does this step take in turn? This step-by-step approach to the goal is essential in order to carry out all the necessary steps, not to disregard anything important and to stand there successfully at the end.

Example: Nina establishes a hierarchy

Let's now relate the ranking of goals to an example. The example will be used throughout much of this chapter to adequately demonstrate how to bring your list of goals to completion in long-term planning. Nina has set 10 goals for herself. She has not necessarily formulated the goals precisely, but she has a sufficiently concrete idea of them:

- Lose 20 kilogram
- Stop smoking
- Earn more money
- Take more time for the family (parents and her 2 brothers)
- Gain more general knowledge
- Travel more often
- Try something new more often
- Create order at home
- Find steady friend
- Do more sports

Nina has noticed so far that quitting smoking and dieting are not compatible. In a way, they are conflicting goals. Because imagine how difficult it is to quit 2 vices at the same time: Giving up both smoking and snacking immediately and simultaneously is a strong imposition on one's will. For the time being, Nina has therefore decided on the diet that is more important to her.

Continue with the other goals: Nina can pursue the desires for more general knowledge and more money simultaneously through distance learning, which is why she makes them complementary goals.

Nina also promotes her diet through sports.

Who knows – maybe she'll find the steady boyfriend she longs for while playing sports? So, Nina decides not to prioritize the goal of finding a boyfriend.

She makes more time for her family by taking smaller day trips with her parents and brothers. For this purpose, she uses 2 weekend days per month and the holidays during the year. On these few days, she takes a break from distance learning to allow herself enough rest.

Thus, she has set the goals and defined which goals she will tackle first and which she will put off for now. She also considers the following ranking of goals:

Overall objective	Interim target	Subgoal	Stage destination
Lose 20 kg and do more sports	Have lost 10 kg by the end of the sixth month	From the tenth week enroll in the gym and lose half a kilogram per week	Lose half a kilogram every week; initially through a change in diet
Higher earnings and more general knowledge	Complete distance learning and apply for new job	Complete first semester on schedule within six months	Start with distance learning to gain qualifications for a better paying job, and set aside 2

			hours each evening to study
Take more time for family, travel more often, and try new things	After 6 months, take a multi-day trip or vacation with the family for the first time and make the vacation rich in experiences and activities	Make concrete plans for 2 weekend days -> The motto is to spend time together outside of the usual environment and with new activities if possible.	Discuss 2 weekend days off with family members each month
Create order at home	After 6 months, if necessary, muck out on 1 or 2 days off.	Do household chores for half an hour every day –1 hour after returning from work; 1 hour each on weekend days.	Getting into the habit of always hanging up clothes after returning home, doing the dishes immediately after a meal, and otherwise cleaning up any messes that have been made right away
Find steady friend	If there is no success for 2 years, reconsider planning and seek advice.	If the stage goal didn't work, try classic places for singles to go (e.g., speed	First do all the other things; because already through gym, distance

		dating, special events, bars)	learning and traveling you can meet people
Stop smoking	After the 3 months, use lower-dose nicotine products and wean off slowly	Use nicotine gum, patches, or other special products and reduce amount of cigarettes smoked during first 3 months of cessation	If health permits, then do not start smoking cessation until 2 years after the successful diet, so that no "addiction shift" occurs

What is Nina doing with her ranking?

On the one hand, she sets complementary goals (lose 20 kg and exercise). On the other hand, she makes goals complementary by making her planning specific: For example, higher earnings and more general knowledge are not necessarily complementary goals. However, by doing distance learning, she makes the goals complementary. This is because the study program provides her with the desired general knowledge through the large number of interdisciplinary modules and insights into other subject areas, while the bachelor's degree enables her to pursue a profession with higher earnings.

In addition to skillfully choosing complementary goals (she combines a total of 7 goals into 3 goals), she postpones other goals. This is evident in finding a steady boyfriend and quitting smoking. In the case of quitting smoking, she notes a conflicting nature with losing weight. In themselves, the 2 need not be mutually exclusive, but if Nina were to do both at the same time, she would have to cope with various cuts from one day to the next – at least that's how she lays it out for herself argumentatively. The advantage of this plan is that she can "enjoy" smoking for 2 more years and put less pressure on herself in setting her goal. With the goal of finding a boyfriend, she initially refrains from clear planning. This is because she recognizes the spontaneity behind this goal: *when* you meet a man can be difficult or impossible to control. True love, which is what Nina is looking for, cannot be forced. So, she realizes that she may already meet her future steady boyfriend while doing new sports activities, meeting her family, or traveling. In case this is not the case, she has formulated a few "contingency plans" in the intermediate goal and sub-goal.

Nina trades off the goal of creating order in the household and keeping it tidy with small windows of time. If you look at it soberly, this is exactly the right choice. Because if you constantly keep things tidy and immediately put them in the right place, wash the dishes or start the vacuum cleaner, you won't usually have to spend much more than 30 minutes a day tidying up.

Overall, by combining several complementary or potentially complementary goals and deferring 2 of them, Nina is only working on 8 desired goals at a time. Since she combines almost all of the goals in some way with at least 1 other goal, it feels like Nina is only working on 4 goals at a time. At the same time, she is pursuing commitments such as her job. In parallel, she integrates social contacts into her life through family and sports. By being mostly free on weekends, she creates plenty of relaxation and space for spontaneity. The time windows that remain for certain obligations (sleeping, eating, hygiene) fit well into the schedule and do not allow stress to arise at all.

What you learn from the example for your planning ...

First and foremost, you learn from Nina's example that pursuing complementary goals offers enormous advantages. You can pursue several goals at once and use your time more efficiently. Goals don't always have to be complementary by themselves. You can make them complementary by choosing actions to achieve them that benefit both goals. This is what Nina did with the goal combination "higher earnings & more general knowledge".

Furthermore, you should not strive to complete all goals as quickly as possible. If you feel no time pressure and have some freedom in prioritizing and completing your goals, then take plenty of time! Nina, for example, has retained the option to readjust in her interim and sub-goals: If she hasn't lost the 10 kilograms after 6 months, she makes a few changes in her planning. You can see this in the table above.

Last tip: Don't assume that everything will run optimally. Those obstacles and problems will occur is absolutely normal and very likely. Nina has understood this. If you do the math, you'll find that with half a kilogram of weight loss per week on her diet, it would by no means take her half a year to lose 10 kilograms. She has left herself almost a whole month as a time buffer, so that if there are problems – especially at the beginning some can occur – she won't jeopardize reaching the intermediate goal. This buffer also has the advantage that if it goes according to plan, she will lose more weight than formulated in the interim goal. This can lead to a positive surprise effect and Nina is most likely more motivated on the way to her goal to also take the 2nd half of the path and lose the additional 10 kilograms.

Task 1

Take your lists of commitments and desired goals from the previous chapters. Rank each goal: How finely do you divide each goal so that you can easily work through its stages and stay motivated? Also create a ranking for the desired goals that you have postponed and do not write on your agenda for the time being. Because later you will come back to your desired goals. Then it is practical to have the appropriate ranking directly.

Time reference of goals

You are already familiar with the classification of goals according to their time reference from the 1st step of the book. It was relevant to introduce this aspect earlier. Feel free to reread the section because the contents are very important for long-term planning. Then continue at this point with your lists and the following example.

Example: Nina sets a time reference

A classification of the goals by time reference, as in the following example, can of course make sense *before* the ranking is determined. However, the approach chosen in this guidebook is that the ranking is formed first. The reason for this is that the ranking leads to a meticulous and quite meticulously executed subdivision of the overall objectives. In this way, the duration until the goals are achieved can be better estimated.

Let us now look at the example of Nina, how she divides her goals according to time reference and how the previous formation of a ranking helped her in this. She still has her 10 overall goals, from which she summarizes the complementary goals and for which she calculates the following time horizons:

Overall objective	Planned duration	Further notes	Time reference
Lose 20 kilograms and do more sports	1 year and 2 months	Plus, another 4 months to prevent the yoyo effect	medium-term
Higher earnings and more general knowledge	3 years (duration of studies)	After 3 years, likely up to 2 more years to get a better paying job	medium to long term
Take more time for family, travel more often, and try something new more often	1 month for organization	Organize in the first month and maintain regular activities month after month thereafter	short term
Stop smoking	1 year to stop smoking cigarettes; then prevent relapse through new positive habits	Do not start until 2 years after weight reduction	medium to long term
Create order at home	At the latest after 8 months (to have	Start immediately and create a little more	short term

	completely cleaned out)	order every day	
Find steady friend	With a natural approach, something should come up within 2 years	Cannot be planned precisely; intensify efforts only after deadline of 2 years	medium-term

What does Nina do when time-referencing her goals?

After ranking them, she writes down how much time her goals take. If she reads "short-term" in the right column, she knows that she has to check the respective task more closely on a daily or monthly basis. Strictly speaking, this example is incomplete: A good classification by time reference would be for Nina to list all short-term, medium-term, and long-term goals in 3 separate tables. With these 3 tables, it would be possible for her to check the intermediate status in different time windows:

> ➢ For example, Nina would look at the table with the short-term goals every day or every week.
> ➢ For example, she could look at the table with the medium-term goals every month.
> ➢ Last, Nina would look at the long-term goals chart once a year.

With the 3 tables divided by time reference, Nina would have a strict separation of the different time references. She would not be driven crazy by medium-term goals but would regularly enjoy the progress on her short-term goals. In turn, she would look at the medium, and long-term goals at regular, but more widely spaced, intervals in order to monitor the intermediate statuses and to tighten up the short-term goals in good time if there was a threat that the goals would be missed.

When Nina combines all this with visualization, she has the ultimate motivation booster. If you imagine that she checks off the short-term goals, day by day or week by week, draws them in a diagram and thus sees how she has come a few percent closer to the long-term goal again through a few small measures, then you understand that the subdivision of the goals according to time reference in combination with a clear ranking is optimal for staying motivated and consistently getting closer to the big goals with small steps.

What you learn from the example for your plans

Dividing your goals by time helps you to move forward in small steps. If you list all short, medium, and long-term goals in 3 different catalogs (books or notebooks), you have a clear separation. You then look at the list of short-term goals every day or week. As you achieve them on schedule, you can check them off one by one and see how fast you're progressing. This is a psychological trick: Why keep looking at the long road to the big goals? Why get discouraged by the many tasks that lie ahead? By working through the short-term and easier goals, you'll move forward much more easily and lightheartedly.

Task 2

You, too, plan according to the time reference of goals. It is best to set up 3 catalogs as described. The 1st catalog concerns short-term goals, the 2nd medium-term goals and the 3rd long-term goals. Create the catalogs and determine for yourself how regularly you want to look into a catalog. It is obvious to look into the catalog with short-term goals in short intervals (e.g., every week). And then? Well, then you'd better start directly with the pursuit of your goals according to your planning! Why wait when your dreams are within reach?

Subdivision according to target importance

The target meanings have some parallels to the time reference. Here, there is a division into strategic, tactical, and operational goals. **Strategic goals** are the long-term goals that are **formulated rather generally**: Improving your income situation, getting your first property, etc. They are fundamental to your overall life. Depending on what your strategy is – making a career, being a family man, helping other people, etc. – you set the strategic goals and formulate them based on the tactical goals.

Tactical goals usually concern the medium-term time horizon. They **summarize which activities are necessary to achieve the strategic goals**. You can get a good impression of this from the examples mentioned above. If your strategic goal is to get a better job with a higher salary, your tactical goal with a medium-term time horizon is to study or train to achieve that goal.

Last but not least, there are the **operational goals**, which are both short, and long-term in nature. On the one hand, they are there to carry out your current mandatory program of work and other commitments. In addition, the **operational goals detail the medium-term goals, which will help you achieve the medium-term goals and thus get closer to the long-term goals**. To follow up on the previous example, in order to complete your studies and find a better job later on, it is necessary to enroll in a university and start studying in a timely manner.

Hint!

What is the actual connection between all the presented subdivisions of goals according to time horizon, goal significance and ranking? The connection between all these things is that they make adequate goal planning possible in the first place. You have strategic goals in life to bring you closer to your dreams? These goals are long-term. It is necessary to divide them into tactical goals and to operationalize them. In other words, you set operational short, and medium-term goals in order to act in a goal-oriented way. Ranking the goals helps you check off one task at a time, motivate yourself, and keep at it. If you follow through with the steps and stay on schedule, your tactics will work so that you achieve the medium-term goals and consistently move toward the long-term goals. Also, if you go through all of these things in your long-term planning and break down all of the goals by time horizon, goal importance, and ranking, you'll notice any inconsistencies. In this way, you realize that you may have missed some important aspects. Consequently, you correct your objectives.

Monitor regularly, evaluate, and change if necessary

Of course, you need an overview of your goals. Because let's be frank and honest: Even with the greatest motivation, you may overlook individual goals. To prevent this from happening and to ensure that you proceed according to plan, there are 3 main methods for monitoring:

➢ Handwritten on a piece of paper or in a book

➢ Use of specialized apps

➢ Use of comprehensive programs (e.g., project management)

We have handwritten your goals and monitored them in almost every task in the book up to this point. The reason you use pen and paper is scientifically based: It causes people to think more carefully about what they write. They select better and accordingly think more carefully about the content. This helps you to think more intensively each time about whether you really want the respective goals.

In addition to handwritten recording, you are free to use digital helpers to record and monitor your goals. Because people tend to use a lot of digital applications every day, I recommend the handwritten version. One thing is clear about this: if you write out all the goals and write complete sentences, it's going to take a lot of effort on your part. That's why a trend has emerged in recent years around the so-called *bullet journal*. You can find all imaginable and important information about this way of keeping a diary and recording your daily tasks at the URL "https://bulletjournal.com/". The author Ryder Carroll has even written a comprehensive book on this topic. The trick to his way of recording tasks and goals in writing is to work with different types of **bullet points,** which make everything clearer and easier and saves time.

Task 3

The choice is yours: either find out how the *bullet journal* works and try it out on your goals. Or come up with your own way to make it easy to handwrite and monitor your goals. After all, writing out your goals in complete sentences and keeping up with them on a daily or weekly basis is exhausting in the long run. Also, when documenting your goals, use your energies sparingly and make it easy rather than difficult.

As a contrast to the handwritten approach, there are the digital helpers. Apps for the smartphone and desktop applications for stationary PCs are plentiful. Because there is an oversupply, it is difficult to find good programs. I myself have only worked with one application, but on a daily basis, as a supplement to handwriting my goals: Asana. It is a program that can be used on the PC and laptop as well as on smaller devices. I always used it on the laptop and the smartphone. This way I always had an overview of all my tasks and goals at home and on the road. The handy thing is that you can create multiple projects. For example, one project can be named "Personal Life" and the other can be named "Career". This is a rough subdivision under which you can list your more detailed goals. It's best to look at the program yourself and find your own way to use it. Because there are various ways to create projects and thus subdivide the goals. The program itself lists in table form, and on a project-to-project basis, indicates which tasks are still to be carried out and which goals they are subordinate to.

Another list of useful apps can be found in the book *Richtig priorisieren* (2014). If necessary, you can also try them out. Some of them specialize in individual functions. Here are 5 promising apps:

- ➤ *Things* for iPhone and iPad users to manage themselves
- ➤ *aTimeLogger* a time tracking app for the iPhone

- ➤ *AWD Time Logger* a time tracking app for devices with the Android system
- ➤ *Eisenhower* as an app for the iPhone to set priorities
- ➤ *Tenplustwo* as a stopwatch app with great utility for unloved tasks (after 10 minutes of work time always comes 2 minutes of break)

Apart from handwritten journals and apps, there is another method of monitoring, which at the same time is highly valued in personal development. This is the visualization method: You already learned about it in *Task 2* from the *Step 1* chapter in this book. Use this method especially for the goals you don't like. The visualizations will keep you better motivated and in a better mood. One possible visualization would be the *progress pie*. It is best to hang visualizations clearly visible on a wall in your home.

Finally, one important question remains: how and when do you change something about your goals?

This is exactly what monitoring is for: to change the objectives if necessary. The central problem with changing goals is that one is not always quite sure whether the goals are being changed rightly or whether it is the wrong decision. It often happens that people pursue their goals well and consistently, but still abandon them. Then it is said that it was too difficult. But was it really?

There is no general formula for when goals should be abandoned. Obviously, you should not pursue goals that you don't care about or that don't do us a reasonable favor that would justify the effort. Pursuing such false goals should not happen anyway if you follow the advice and guidance in this guide. Now, it is possible that even if you follow the right goals and the instructions in this guidebook, at some point you may feel the urge to change individual goals ...

It's permissible and important to make changes when you realize you have too hard a workload. Especially in the 1st few weeks of new goal setting, it is not uncommon to realize that you've taken on a bit too much. Slowing down the pace now is helpful. Either you eliminate less important goals, or you reduce the pace.

Another situation in which objectives change is changes in one's own character, certain ways of thinking, and life circumstances. A prime example of this is provided by author Eric Adler in his work *More of Life* (2014): A person sets himself the goal of being the most successful representative of his company. On the way to this goal, he meets a woman with whom he begins a relationship. With this acquaintance, the focus in his life shifts abruptly. In such situations, it is also not wrong to change one's own goals or, under certain circumstances, to cancel them completely.

This is not the end of the situations that justify changing or canceling goals: there are goals that you take up even though you are not sure that they really fit you and the situation in your life. Even reading this guide and following all the helpful advice, you may find yourself uncertain about your future. In that case, the tip is: try everything that appeals to you in the slightest. Try new things. Sometimes it is only possible by trying and observing. Find out by doing which goals suit you and which do not. Have the courage to break off goals and set new ones if something doesn't appeal to you on the 1st attempt. Important: Don't break off at the 1st hurdle, but patiently give it a chance.

I hope these few hints can help you figure out when you should and shouldn't break goals. Basically, though, there is no general formula. You'll have to intuitively decide for yourself when it's appropriate to change goals. However, keep in mind that if you are more than 50% of the way there, or if your goals are costing you a lot (e.g., distance learning), you should only abandon them in the most extreme cases.

Final task

If you have completed the tasks in this chapter, the long-term planning is already done, and your goals are set. Ideally, you have already started tracking your goals. What could the final task be about? Now it gets interesting with regard to your environment: Given that all your goals are in place, you can talk to those around you about your objectives, get opinions and, if necessary, redesign the environment. Ask what people think of your goals. You can accept constructive criticism and make changes. If you have completely new goals in life, try to make new inspiring acquaintances related to your respective goals.

Closing words

Each reader writes their own story. You have the piece of paper, the pencil, and a set of ideas. Now you decide which story you want to write. Your goals will be based on that. Do you want to write the story of a career person who has extensive know-how and is self-actualized in his work? Do you want to reach people and spread your views? Does your heart, beat for your family and do you define your life by their happiness?

Whatever path you choose: You can walk it and achieve all your goals, as long as you set them realistically and ensure a certain balance. Every person needs this balance in his life. Not everything can revolve around one goal if you don't want to miss out on too much in your life. This is how scientists, psychologists, needs researchers and many other groups of people who have something to say in the field of personal development and goal setting see it. Therefore, the biggest takeaway from this guidebook is that, as different as we may be, at our core we all have the same needs and require the same components in life. These include existential needs, physical and mental well-being, a social environment, and the opportunity for self-actualization. How much of these things we need, however, is an individual matter.

Think about what you consider important in your life. Create a careful plan with goals according to the instructions in this book. Because setting and pursuing goals without a plan is almost impossible. Unfortunately, a surprising number of people take such a path. Consequently, they stray in some areas of life or even in their entire life. They do not get the most out of their lives. Sometimes talents remain unused, sometimes people even go astray out of desperation. Some might have had the chance to make a positive mark on entire nations or even the world, but let their lives pass aimlessly.

In our childhood, there is usually no need for a plan, because a large part of life is determined by others. The school, with its curriculum and teachers as the enforcers, provides us with one framework, while parents, with their upbringing, provide the other. Already here we can see that when parents let the leash loose, it is not uncommon for children to neglect their school duties and fail to achieve the goals there. When one part in a person's system is not functioning, interactions occur that can also negatively affect other parts. So already in childhood it becomes clear how finely and closely the system "human & environment" works. In adulthood it is then exactly the same issue, only that you have to take more responsibility yourself.

Have the courage to take responsibility by setting your own goals. This is probably the greatest challenge: leaving your comfort zone and making your own decisions. It is all too likely that mistakes will be made in the process. After all, a lifetime is long, and especially in anyone's early 20s, experience is limited. But at least they will be your mistakes – they will be your hallmark, and you will be able to tell about them later to help or warn other people. Besides, each mistake lowers the probability that you will make more mistakes. Finally, you learn.

Think about what adjustments you would like to make in your life. Who knows – maybe thanks to this guide you'll realize that you already have everything you want? In the pursuit of more, many an ambitious person has noticed that it doesn't really have to be more. So don't let yourself be blinded by certain ambitions within yourself but take into account the big picture in everything – within yourself and in what affects you from the outside. I wish you so much luck with this!

References and further reading

Literature Sources:

Adler, E.: *Mehr vom Leben – Die 12 Naturgesetze zum Erfolg©.*
München: Südwest Verlag, 2014.

Hollywood, C.: *Wer will, der kann! Wie du deine Ziele schneller und
einfacher erreichst.* Heidelberg: dpunkt.verlag GmbH, 2018.

Moestl, B.: *Der Weg des Tigers.* München: Knaur Verlag, 2013.

Proske, H.; Reichert, J. F.; Reiff, E.: Richtig priorisieren.
Freiburg: Haufe-Lexware GmbH & Co. KG, 2014.

Schmidbauer, W.: *Die gelassene Art, Ziele zu erreichen! Abschied vom
Erfolgszwang.* Freiburg im Breisgau: KREUZ VERLAG,
2012.

Online sources:

Asendorpf, J. B.; Banse, R.; Wilpers, S.; Neyer, F. J.: Diagnostica
1997,43, Heft 4, 289:313, *Beziehungsspezifische
Bindungsskalen für Erwachsene und ihre Validierung durch
Netzwerk- und Tagebuchverfahren.* Göttingen: Hogrefe-
Verlag, 1997, von https://www.psychologie.hu-
berlin.de/de/prof/per/downloads/Bindungsskalen.pdf

Carroll, R.: The Bullet Journal Merthod, von
https://bulletjournal.com/.

Clauß, M.; Kern, C.: Südwest Presse, *Multi-Millionärin durch Aktien: „Börsen-Oma" aus Ulm ist tot.* (29. September 2020). https://www.swp.de/suedwesten/staedte/ulm/beate-sander-ulm-tod-burch-krebs-vermoegen-boerse-boersen-oma-aktien-millionen-51893466.html

Deutsche Gesellschaft für Ernährung e. V., *Vollwertig essen und trinken nach den 10 Regeln der DGE.* (Download vom 25.02.2021, 19:44 Uhr). https://www.dge.de/ernaehrungspraxis/vollwertige-ernaehrung/10-regeln-der-dge/.

Müller, T.: ÄrzteZeitung, *Wer sechs bis acht Stunden pro Nacht schläft, lebt am längsten.* (28. Dezember 2018). https://www.aerztezeitung.de/Medizin/Wer-sechs-bis-acht-Stunden-pro-Nacht-schlaeft-lebt-am-laengsten-232317.html

Ries, F.: https://www.fabianries.de/. *Das Lebensrestaurant.* (1. November 2015). https://lebensrestaurant.de/lebensrestaurant-geschichte/

Schmermund, K.: Forschung & Lehre, *Warum wir wieder mehr mit der Hand schreiben sollten.* (04.02.2020). https://www.forschung-und-lehre.de/forschung/warum-wir-wieder-mehr-mit-der-hand-schreiben-sollten-2504/

Stanzl, E.: Wiener Zeitung .at, *Was die Handschrift im Gehirn bewirkt.* (10.02.2015).

https://www.wienerzeitung.at/nachrichten/wissen/men
sch/734175-Was-die-Handschrift-im-Gehirn-
bewirkt.html

Washington, D.: YouTube-Channel von AlexKaltsMotivation, *WATCH THIS EVERYDAY AND CHANGE YOUR LIFE - Denzel Washington Motivational Speech 2020.* (Download vom 25.02.2021, 19:50 Uhr). https://www.youtube.com/watch?v=tbnzAVRZ9Xc&t =260s.

Weiss, B.: Der Tagesspiegel, Einsamkeit macht Menschen krank. (01.09.2012). https://www.tagesspiegel.de/wissen/psychologie-einsamkeit-macht-menschen-krank/7080868.html

ZSH GmbH, *Effizient lernen: die vier besten Lerntechniken für Zahnmedizin-Studenten.* (23. Juni 2020). https://www.zsh.de/blog/lerntechniken-zahnmedizin-studenten#_Toc42861265

Printed in Great Britain
by Amazon

16033714R00078